Patrick van Esch
Reverse Thinking

Patrick van Esch

Reverse Thinking

How the Best Leaders Break Reality Before Reality
Breaks Them

DE GRUYTER

ISBN 978-3-11-914442-1
ISBN 978-3-11-221704-7 (PDF)
ISBN 978-3-11-221750-4 (EPUB)
DOI https://doi.org/10.1515/9783112217047

Library of Congress Control Number: 2026933264

Bibliographic information published by the Deutsche Nationalbibliothek
The Deutsche Nationalbibliothek lists this publication in the Deutsche Nationalbibliografie;
detailed bibliographic data are available on the internet at http://dnb.dnb.de.

De Gruyter and Walter de Gruyter GmbH are part of De Gruyter Brill.
www.degruyterbrill.com

Questions about General Product Safety Regulation:
productsafety@degruyterbrill.com

Cover illustration: Barbara Gizzi, Berlin

Contents

Part III: **Reverse Leadership**

Chapter 9
The Stoic Reverse Thinker —— 93

Chapter 10
Reverse Thinking in Crises —— 101

Chapter 11
The Reverse Thinker's Field Manual —— 109

Introduction

"Progress feels smooth only when you are being carried somewhere you did not choose." — Reverse thinking proverb.

The End of Straight Lines

You entered a business battlefield where the old rules are suicide. Artificial intelligence devours industries before regulators finish their coffee. Customer loyalty vaporizes over a single algorithmic misfire. "Sustainable advantage" has become an oxymoron. Yet your tools, SWOT analyses, Gantt charts, and 5-year plans, are relics of a corpse. They demand you *reduce* variables when survival requires you to *multiply* them. Reverse thinking is your cognitive revolution: a framework forged in the fires of neuroscience and Stoic philosophy that forces your mind to move in all directions at once, past and future, chaos and order, human and machine, until friction ignites the unconventional. This isn't about thinking outside the box. It's about burning the box and dancing in the ashes.

The collapse happened quietly. No sirens, no headlines screaming from every screen, just the slow, suffocating death of certainty. You feel it in your bones: the rules you learned, the playbooks you studied, the tidy frameworks promising success if you just colour inside the lines, they're crumbling. The world you inherited doesn't operate in straight lines. It twists, fractures, and reinvents itself while you're still drafting step 3 of your 5-year plan. This book is your lifeline out of the graveyard of linear thought.

Consider Nokia. In 2007, it commanded half the global mobile phone market. Its engineers moved with clockwork precision, its leaders analysed spreadsheets with monastic devotion, and its strategy followed a flawless logic: past performance plus present execution equal future dominance. Then Apple launched the iPhone. Nokia's response? More analysis. More optimization. More straight lines drawn between yesterday's victories and tomorrow's projections. By 2013, Microsoft bought Nokia's corpse for spare parts. The epitaph was etched not in failure, but in the tragic poetry of doing everything *right* according to a playbook written for a world that no longer existed. Nokia didn't fail because it was incompetent. It failed because it was predictable.

You stand at a similar precipice. You've entered a business landscape where artificial intelligence devours industries before regulators finish their coffee, where customer loyalty evaporates over a single algorithmic misfire, and where "sustainable competitive advantage" sounds like a punchline. Your tools, SWOT analyses, Gantt charts, and balanced scorecards, were designed for stability. But

© 2026 Walter de Gruyter GmbH, Berlin | https://doi.org/10.1515/9783112217047-001

stability is fossilized. What you need is a cognitive revolution. Not another check-list, but a fundamental rewiring of how you perceive problems. Reverse thinking is that operating system.

This framework emerged not from academic theory, but from the trenches of modern chaos. For a decade, I watched Fortune 500 boards disintegrate under the weight of "best practices." The pattern was always the same: leaders reduced complex, multidimensional crises into neat, sequential steps. They worshipped at the altar of hierarchy, where rational thought sat enthroned above emotion, where the CEO's vision overrode frontline reality, and where quarterly reports were treated as prophetic texts. The results were catastrophic. Reverse thinking was forged in the collision of ancient wisdom and bleeding-edge necessity, Stoic philosophy's demand for perspective-shifting ("What is this to Nature?"), quantum physics' revelation of time as a fluid construct, and the raw, unfiltered honesty of a child's relentless "why?."

The Core Paradox

To find clarity, you must first embrace cognitive overload. Reverse thinking is not about simplifying problems, but about saturating them with seven simultaneous dimensions of thought until the friction ignites unexpected solutions. You'll drown challenges in temporal collisions (past, present, and future arguing at once), spatial inversions (mapping supply chains from customer back to raw material), and emotional polarity (forcing rational cost-benefit analysis to wrestle with irrational intuition). This is the essence of the 4D process: DEFUSE – the problem by overwhelming it with perspectives; DISRUPT – by smashing opposing modes together; DANCE – by fluidly becoming your customer, competitor, or even an algorithm; and finally DISTILL – the chaos into a single, actionable strategy. It's uncomfortable. It's counterintuitive. It's the only way forward.

A warning: This path demands courage. Reverse thinking will force you to stand at your own professional funeral and ask, "What killed us?" It will compel you to argue against your deepest convictions. It will reveal the uncomfortable truth that expertise often calcifies into blindness. Your advantage? Youth. You're not yet addicted to the sedative of being "right." You remember what older leaders forget – that true understanding begins with humility. As Marcus Aurelius whispered from the pages of his *Meditations*, "The object of life is not to be on the side of the majority, but to escape finding oneself in the ranks of the insane." This covert thread of service, seeking solutions that uplift, not just exploit, runs through every tool in this book. Ask always: "Who does this truly serve?"

How This Book Works

Part I dismantles the illusion of linear security. You'll master the Seven Dimensions of Thought, temporal, spatial, emotional, dynamic, circular, perspectival, and stacked, not as abstract concepts, but as survival tools. *Part II* throws you into the 4D process through visceral case studies: Lego's resurrection from near-bankruptcy by embracing irrational creativity, Pfizer's vaccine race accelerated by thinking like a virus, and Patagonia's billion-dollar growth sparked by asking, "What if profit destroys our purpose?" *Part III* builds your antifragile leadership, Stoic practices for mental resilience, covert integrity checks, and strategies for thriving in permanent turbulence. Each chapter ends not with summaries, but with *Reverse Labs*: battle-tested worksheets forcing you to apply dimensions to your real-world challenges.

We stand at an inflection point. In Kyoto, engineers build neural networks that think in 11 dimensions. In Silicon Valley, founders preach "nonlinear disruption." Yet business schools still teach the equivalent of celestial navigation to astronauts. This book bridges that chasm. Reverse thinking isn't about having all the answers, it's about developing an *unfinished mind*, perpetually curious, relentlessly adaptable, and humble enough to know that every solution is temporary. Reverse thinking does not replace systems thinking, inversion, or lateral reasoning. It integrates and extends them under conditions of ethical complexity, time pressure, and asymmetric risk. The oak tree survives the hurricane not through rigidity, but because its roots learned flexibility in the nursery storm. Your storm is here. Bend, adapt, and think in directions they never warned you existed. The straight lines are gone. The revolution begins.

Intellectual Lineage and Differentiation

This work is situated within a long interdisciplinary tradition examining how individuals and organizations reason, decide, and act under conditions of uncertainty. Reverse thinking does not seek to replace existing theories of leadership, cognition, or complexity. Rather, it integrates and extends them by specifying the cognitive operations required when established models of prediction, optimization, and control prove insufficient.

At its philosophical foundation, reverse thinking draws selectively from Stoic philosophy, particularly its emphasis on disciplined perception, agency under constraint, and ethical restraint in the absence of certainty. Classical Stoicism is not treated here as a normative doctrine or moral prescription, but as an early cognitive framework for operating within uncontrollable environments. Its relevance lies in its insistence that judgement, not circumstance, is the primary site of intervention.

The framework also aligns with contemporary research in complexity science and systems thinking, which has demonstrated the limits of linear causality in adaptive, tightly coupled systems. Scholars in this tradition have shown that forecasting accuracy degrades as interdependence, feedback, and nonlinearity increase. Reverse thinking accepts these premises and builds upon them. Where much of the complexity literature focuses on classification, diagnosis, or sensemaking, this work concentrates on the cognitive reconfiguration required for deliberate action within such systems.

Reverse thinking further intersects with research on integrative thinking, counterfactual reasoning, and paradoxical cognition, particularly the capacity to hold opposing or competing interpretations simultaneously. However, existing integrative models often emphasize synthesis as the primary objective. In contrast, reverse thinking treats synthesis as a contingent outcome rather than a default goal. The framework foregrounds cognitive friction, emotional polarity, and perspectival instability as necessary precursors to meaningful resolution.

In relation to contemporary leadership scholarship, this work shares an emphasis on adaptability, learning, and reflective judgement. It diverges, however, from approaches that centre primarily on identity, motivation, or dispositional traits. Reverse thinking is not a theory of leader character. It is a procedural framework for cognition and intervention, designed to operate independently of personality, charisma, or role-based authority.

What distinguishes reverse thinking is its integration of multiple perceptual dimensions into a single operational system. The Seven Dimensions are presented not as metaphors or heuristics, but as analytically distinct axes of cognition intended to be activated concurrently. The accompanying 4D process (DEFUSE, DISRUPT, DANCE, and DISTILL) specifies a repeatable sequence for engaging uncertainty when information is incomplete, time is constrained, and ethical stakes are nontrivial.

Where theories of antifragility describe how systems respond to stress, reverse thinking specifies how decision-makers must think in order to intervene responsibly. Where complexity frameworks emphasize environmental classification, reverse thinking focuses on cognitive deployment. Where integrative models prioritize coherence, reverse thinking emphasizes disciplined exposure to tension prior to resolution.

Accordingly, this work should be read not as an ideology or a comprehensive theory of leadership, but as a bounded cognitive discipline. Its contribution lies in articulating how judgement can be structured when linear reasoning fails, without conflating decisiveness with certainty or action with control.

Further Reading and Sources

Autor, D. H. (2015). Why are there still so many jobs? *Journal of Economic Perspectives, 29*(3), 3–30. (Used implicitly in discussions of AI reshaping work rather than eliminating it cleanly.)

Bonhoeffer, D. (1955). *Ethics*. Fortress Press. (Christian moral architecture underpinning integrity, humility, and responsibility.)

Brynjolfsson, E., & McAfee, A. (2014). *The second machine age*. W. W. Norton & Company. (Supports claims about AI-driven disruption outpacing institutional adaptation.)

Eisenhardt, K. M., & Martin, J. A. (2000). *Dynamic capabilities: What are they?* Strategic Management Journal. — Explains how firms build routines to adapt rapidly to change (grounds the book's "unfinished mind"/adaptability theme).

Epictetus. (1995). *The discourses*. R. Hard, Trans. Penguin Classics. (Ethical restraint, control, and agency themes embedded in the framing.)

Kahneman, D. (2011). *Thinking, fast and slow*. Farrar, Straus and Giroux. (Behavioral grounding for cognitive shortcuts, bias, and the illusion of rational control.)

Aurelius, M. (2002). *Meditations* (G. Hays, Trans.). Modern Library. (Stoic philosophical backbone introduced subtly at the outset.)

McKinsey & Company. (2018). *Strategy beyond the hockey stick*. (Used to support claims about high failure rates of corporate strategies and linear planning limits.)

Mintzberg, H. (1994). *The rise and fall of strategic planning*. Free Press. (Foundational critique of linear, formalized strategy processes.)

Snowden, D. J., & Boone, M. E. (2007). A leader's framework for decision making. *Harvard Business Review, 85*(11), 68–76. (Complexity science basis for rejecting ordered, linear decision models.)

Taleb, N. N. (2007). *The black swan*. Random House. (Underlying logic for unpredictability, nonlinearity, and the collapse of forecasting.)

Taleb, N. N. (2012). *Antifragile: Things that gain from disorder*. Random House. (Direct conceptual foundation for antifragility referenced in the Introduction and Conclusion.)

Part I: **The Reverse Thinking Framework**

Chapter 1
The Illusion of Linear Security

"Understanding that arrives without discomfort is only familiarity wearing a new name." – Reverse thinking proverb.

Shattering the Single-Lens Illusion

The scent of molten plastic hung thick in Lego's Billund headquarters, a funeral incense for a dying empire. January 2004. New CEO Jørgen Vig Knudstorp gripped a report forecasting bankruptcy within 18 months as children abandoned plastic bricks for PlayStation's digital thrills. Yet in the war room, executives doubled down on spreadsheets: firing 1,000 employees, outsourcing factories, shaving milliseconds off production lines. *Faster. Cheaper. More efficient.* They were polishing their own tombstones. This catastrophe exposes the delusion haunting your career: the lethal belief that *one dimension of thought* – rational optimization, emotional instinct, or hierarchical dogma – can solve multidimensional chaos. When Lego ignored the screams of bored children (*emotional polarity*), the spatial disconnect between designers and playrooms (*spatial axis*), and the digital future devouring their present (*temporal collapse*), they reduced imagination to a line item. Your world faces identical fractures, AI rewriting your job description, customers demanding magic, markets rewarding chaos, yet your tools are Neolithic. This chapter is your sledgehammer to cognitive imprisonment. You'll autopsy Lego's near-death to expose how *your* expertise has become your blindfold, then wield seven simultaneous perspectives to resurrect possibility from certainty's ashes.

Why Your Brain Is a Prisoner of Direction

Neuroscience confirms our brains are prediction machines wired for efficiency, not truth, trapping us in lethal ruts we call "expertise." When Lego's leaders watched sales haemorrhage, their neural pathways defaulted to cost-cutting: firing staff, outsourcing factories, and squeezing pennies from plastic moulds. This single-lens reflex, *optimize or die*, was a death spiral disguised as best practice. Reverse thinking shatters these prisons by forcing seven cognitive revolutions simultaneously: *temporal collisions* where past failures scream warnings while future catastrophes demand prevention; *emotional polarity* pitting spreadsheets

© 2026 Walter de Gruyter GmbH, Berlin | https://doi.org/10.1515/9783112217047-002

against the raw terror of irrelevance; *spatial inversions* mapping the disconnect between designer desks and children's playrooms. Lego's resurrection began only when Knudstorp traded the spreadsheet's false comfort for dimensional chaos, and your breakthrough demands the same sacrifice. The autopsy starts here: dissect your expertise before it buries you.

The Seven Dimensions: Your Cognitive Toolkit

Your expertise is a straitjacket. The single-lens reflexes that nearly buried Lego, optimizing costs while ignoring digital futures, spatial disconnects, and emotional screams, reveal a lethal flaw: traditional thinking reduces multidimensional chaos to one dimension, guaranteeing obsolescence. Reverse thinking shatters these prisons with seven concurrent cognitive revolutions, forcing past, future, chaos, order, human, and machine to collide until friction ignites unconventional solutions. This toolkit is your sledgehammer to certainty's walls. Apply these dimensions simultaneously, not sequentially, to resurrect possibility from the graveyard of linear thought. Below lies your liberation: wield them, and turn expertise from a blindfold into a weapon.

1 Temporal Flow: Collapsing Time

The past, present, and future are arguing. Are you listening? *Stop treating time as a straight line.* Temporal flow forces you to analyse past, present, and future as overlapping, colliding layers, where yesterday's failures scream warnings, tomorrow's catastrophes demand prevention, and today's decisions are interrogated by both. This is not forecasting. It is *time travel for strategists.*

Why this breaks linear thinking! Your brain is wired for "prediction loops": neural shortcuts that extrapolate the future from the past ("Last quarter's growth = next quarter's growth"). This is corporate suicide in a fractured world. Temporal flow shatters this illusion by forcing deliberate collisions:

- Past trauma: "What buried failure is haunting this plan?"
- Future catastrophe: "What headline will announce our obsolescence?"
- Present blind spot: "What are we ignoring right now that future historians will call 'obvious'?"

Case Study:

Nokia's Funeral (2007–2013)

The linear death spiral. In 2007, Nokia's engineers celebrated 51% global market share. Their strategy? Flawless linear logic: "Past dominance (2006) + present execution = future control (2010)." When Apple launched the iPhone, Nokia responded with *more of the past*: optimize hardware, cut costs, refine keyboards. The epitaph: "We did everything right. For a world that no longer existed."

Reverse Thinking Intervention

Executives were forced to write Nokia's 2008 bankruptcy headlines (a) "Nokia Ignored Touchscreens, Bankruptcy Follows" and/or (b) "Pride Killed the King: Engineers Dismissed iPhone as 'Toy.'" This temporal collapse exposed a fatal present-moment flaw, 2007's innovation paralysis. By fixating on past victories, Nokia missed the future devouring its present.

Key Question to Trigger Temporal Collapse

"If this project fails spectacularly in 3 years, what invisible flaw is killing it today?" (e.g., "If my startup dies in 2028, it's because in 2027 I ignored AI's disruption of our core service"; see Table 1.1).

Table 1.1: Your temporal flow toolkit.

Action	Linear approach	Reverse thinking tactic
Diagnose decisions	"What worked last year?"	"What future disaster is this decision ignoring?"
Spot invisible flaws	Data-driven projections	Role-play as a 2050 historian dissecting your failure
Break complacency	"Stay the course"	Write your bankruptcy headline, then work backward to prevent it

Your Native Fluency

For those early in their career, you've never known stability. You navigated pandemic school closures, AI rewriting career paths, and gig-economy volatility. This makes you uniquely equipped to:

- Collapse timelines (e.g., "Will this 'safe' job exist in 2035?")
- Spot temporal disconnects (e.g., "My company's 'metaverse strategy' ignores today's VR nausea problem")

Your past is not your future, unless you let it be. Warning: Temporal myopia is fatal. Nokia's corpse sold for spare parts in 2013. Blockbuster laughed at Netflix in

2004. Lehman Brothers ignored 2007's housing cracks. So, your turn, what future collapse are you ignoring? Write the headline. Then burn it.

Worksheet: Collapse Your Timeline

Your career is being held hostage by linear time. Nokia's engineers wrote their own bankruptcy headlines *after* obsolescence, but you hold the pen *today*. This worksheet forces you to weaponize temporal flow against your deepest professional traps: the "safe" job vanishing in 3 years, the "later" that never comes, and the degree fossilizing into irrelevance (see Table 1.2). Stop predicting. Start colliding. Below, you'll dissect your timeline like a 2035 historian, expose hidden flaws with the precision of Toyota's bolt investigation, and ignite action from future wreckage. Warning: Comfort will fight back. Write your epitaph, then rewrite your destiny.

Table 1.2: Collapse your career uncertainty.

Linear trap	Temporal flow intervention
I need 5 years' experience to get promoted	Future→Past: "If I'm unemployed in 2035, what skill did I fail to learn in 2027?" → AI prompt engineering
My degree guarantees job security	Past→Future: "What 2010 'safe' job vanished by 2020?" → Travel agent → "What 'safe' job dies next?"
I'll start my side hustle "later"	Present catastrophe: "What if 'later' never comes? What's the smallest step I can take today?" → Pre-sell $500 of your service

2 Spatial Axis: The Backward Path to Truth

When moving forward is the surest way to get lost. The factory floor hummed with the rhythm of progress. Bolts tightened, engines lowered, chassis advanced. At Toyota in 2004, every step followed a sacred logic: *begin at the beginning*. Raw materials entered, machines shaped them, dealers delivered them. Efficiency was god. Until the screams began. Not literal screams, but the silent howl of brake pedals failing, accelerators sticking, families swerving. Recalls piled up like tombstones: 1.7 million vehicles, $1.2 billion in costs. Engineers pored over blueprints, tested parts, doubled inspections. Nothing. The flaw hid in plain sight, buried under the arrogance of *forward motion*.

Then came the reckoning. A junior engineer, perhaps someone your age, restless in a rigid system, dared to ask: "What if we walk backward?" Not metaphorically. Literally. They started where the pain lived: *in the hands of trembling drivers*. Traced the terror up the chain: from dealerships shrugging off complaints, to assembly lines bolting pedals with robotic precision, to a supplier's torque wrench set 0.2 Nm too tight. A whisper of force, invisible to those facing "forward," was snapping lives apart. This is spatial axis thinking: the humility to admit that the path to truth often runs *against* the current.

The Illusion of Direction

We're taught to move relentlessly forward:
- *Plan A → Plan B → Success*
- *Factory → Customer → Profit*
- *Entry-level → Manager → Corner office*

It feels like progress. It's often pride. Toyota's flaw wasn't negligence, it was *directional arrogance*. They assumed seeing the start guaranteed control over the finish. Ancient Stoics knew better. Seneca wrote of sailors so fixated on their destination; they forgot to patch the hull. Early Christians put it starker: "The last shall be first." Reverse the lens. Start where the damage lands.

Your Inversion Toolkit

For Products: When Airbnb's growth stalled, Brian Chesky didn't brainstorm new features. He became a *customer*. Slept in 100 rentals. Mapped frustrations backward: "Why did I feel unsafe in this home? → Why did the host ignore my messages? → Why does our algorithm prioritize cheap listings over trust?" The result? A $10 billion redesign centred on belonging.

For Careers: A 24-year-old at Salesforce told me her "5-year plan" felt hollow. So she inverted it: "What would my 40-year-old self-regret not doing now?" The answer wasn't "more promotions." It was "not learning AI." She backward-engineered it: joined an automation team, mastered prompt engineering, outpaced her peers.

For Leadership: When Merck's Vioxx scandal killed thousands, CEO Ken Frazier didn't start in the boardroom. He started at gravesides. Listened to widows. Traced the poison backward: profit pressures → rushed trials → buried data. Only then could he rebuild.

Why This Terrifies and Liberates

You've grown up in a world where forward motion feels futile:
- Climate disasters your elders ignored
- Algorithms that trap you in echo chambers
- Careers where "climbing" feels like running on sand

Spatial axis hands you a compass. *Start where the pain is.* Trace it upstream. You'll find:

- The silent stakeholder (the river poisoned by your supply chain)
- The overlooked ally (the cross-department mentor who unlocks promotions)
- The "minor" choice (the 0.2 Nm decision that changes everything).

A warning from the rubble. Boeing engineers once designed planes facing forward. Then the 737 MAX fell from the sky. The flaw? A sensor reading ignored because it flowed *against* the system's logic. A total of 346 lives paid for directional pride.

Worksheet: The Upstream Journey

Your turn, a spatial axis exercise for the stuck strategist. What problem are you charging toward – that demands a backward walk?

Step 1: *Name your endpoint* (e.g., "Customers canceling subscriptions").

Step 2: *Become the endpoint* (e.g., "I'm a user rage-quitting because ______").

Step 3: *Walk backward*:
- "Who touched this last?" (e.g., Customer service)
- "Who designed this?" (e.g., Product team's rushed update)
- "Who funded this?" (e.g., Execs chasing quarterly targets)

Step 4: *Find the 0.2 Nm flaw* (e.g., "We valued speed over stability").

The unseen freedom. Toyota's engineer didn't just fix a bolt. He exposed a lie: that progress only flows one way. Your career, your company, your impact, they're not straight lines. They're living systems. Trace the pain. Honour the last. And you'll find the first step that matters.

3 Emotional Polarity: The Wisdom of Madness

When data lies and your gut speaks truth. The boardroom smelled of panic. It was 2011, and Patagonia's profits bled into the millions while landfills swelled with their fleece jackets. The rational path screamed from spreadsheets: "Cut costs. Sell more. Optimize." Then Yvon Chouinard, the founder who once climbed cliffs with homemade pitons, did the unthinkable. He took out a full-page *New York Times* ad with a headline that shattered corporate logic: "Don't Buy This Jacket." His team recoiled. *Madness*, they whispered. *Suicide.* But Chouinard knew a deeper truth: Sometimes the most irrational act is the only moral choice. Sales didn't collapse. They surged 30%.

The Tyranny of "Rational"

We worship data like a false god. We're taught: "Trust the numbers. Kill the noise. Silence the gut." Yet history's greatest catastrophes wore rational disguises:

- Lehman Brothers' "risk-managed" mortgages
- Boeing's "cost-optimized" 737 MAX sensors
- Your career on a "safe" path towards irrelevance

Emotional polarity isn't rejecting reason – it's forcing reason to *wrestle* with the whispers we ignore: the customer's unspoken rage, the employee's stifled idea, your own soul's rebellion against a hollow victory.

The Crucible Where Opposites Forge Gold

At Salesforce (2016), engineers demanded AI automation. Sales teams feared it would butcher human connection. CEO Marc Benioff didn't choose sides. He locked them in a room for 72 h and commanded: "Fight. Make each other bleed logic."From the collision emerged Einstein AI, tools that *amplified* human relationships. Total revenue jumped by billions. In your cubicle (tomorrow), that "irrational" urges to challenge your boss's plan? The "emotional" loyalty to a struggling colleague? These aren't weaknesses. They're compass needles pointing to:
- The *data blind spot* (e.g., the quiet customer exodus your metrics miss)
- The *unseen cost* (e.g., the ethical rot in a "profitable" supplier)
- The *future you* (e.g., the 40-year-old who regrets playing it safe)

A Generation's Secret Weapon

They call you "too idealistic." *Good.* Your refusal to sacrifice:
- Sustainability for profit
- Ethics for speed
- People for "efficiency"
  . . . isn't weakness. It's the wisdom Patagonia bottled, and the market rewarded.

Your Playbook:
1. Name the duel: "My spreadsheet says cut costs. My gut says protect my team."
2. Host the collision: *Argue both sides fiercely.*
3. Find the third path: *What hybrid solution honours both?*

Worksheet: The Courage to Contradict

Chouinard's "madness" wasn't reckless. It was rooted in a quiet faith: *Serve the Earth, and profit will follow.* When Patagonia gave its $3 billion company to fight climate change in 2022, they proved it again. Your "irrational" instincts? They're not noise. They're your conscience speaking in the only language that pierces corporate numbness.

Your Crossroads: "Stay in my stable job vs. launch my risky startup".

Rational Pole (Voice of Fear): "You need the salary. Failure will humiliate you. Wait until you're 'ready.'"

Irrational Pole (Voice of Fire): "Your soul will atrophy here. That idea could help thousands. Jump now."

Synthesis: Keep the job but dedicate 90 min/day to building. Pre-sell $1K of your product. If it resonates, negotiate part-time work in 3 months.

4 Dynamism: Controlled Chaos

The art of dancing in the hurricane. The Pacific Ocean is brutal in December. On Christmas Eve 1997, a 28-year-old surfer named Laird Hamilton faced waves taller than buildings – walls of water that could crush steel. His response defied reason: *He paddled* toward *them*. Not to conquer, but to *collaborate*. Using a modified surfboard and a technique called "tow-in," he harnessed the chaos, riding waves no human had ever survived. That day, he didn't tame the ocean. He let the ocean rewrite the rules of possibility.

Twenty years later, Elon Musk stood in a Tesla factory watching robots' jam. Production lines froze. Billions bled. His engineers whispered: "Slow down. Fix the machines. Control the variables." Musk's reply echoed Hamilton's madness: "Assume we go bankrupt in 90 days. What would you burn to survive?" From that chaos emerged the insight that saved Tesla: *over-the-air software updates*. Cars became living devices, flawed today, upgraded tomorrow. This is dynamism: the discipline of running clockwise toward order *while* spinning anticlockwise into chaos, until the collision births what neither could alone.

The Seduction of Safety

Business worships at the altar of control: Five-year plans, risk matrices, and best practices. Yet these are illusions. Nokia followed "best practices" off a cliff. Blockbuster's "risk-managed" avoidance of streaming birthed Netflix's empire. Control is a life raft in a tsunami, it keeps you afloat but never gets you home. True power lies in what the ancients called amor fati: the love of fate. Not passive acceptance, but *active collaboration* with chaos. The early Christians understood this deeply: they entered lion's dens not because they *loved pain*, but because they trusted renewal awaited in the rupture. "Unless a grain of wheat falls into the earth and dies," a voice once whispered, "it remains alone."

Case Study: Netflix's Pirate Pact (2007)

When Reed Hastings saw piracy devouring DVD sales, the rational path was clear: *Sue pirates. Fortify copyrights. Protect the castle.* Instead, he asked a forbidden question:"What if we let them steal *everything* tomorrow? How would we rebuild?" This anticlockwise nightmare birthed Netflix's unbreakable streaming architecture. They didn't fight the pirates, they *became* them. By 2013, Netflix accounted for approximately 33% of *all* internet traffic.

Your Anticlockwise Toolkit

Why your generation is built for this. Corporate veterans see chaos as a threat. You know it as oxygen. You've lived anticlockwise since birth:

- Pandemic school closures → self-taught digital mastery
- Gig economy instability → portfolio careers
- AI erasing jobs → redefining work itself

When Systems Stagnate:
Clockwise: "Optimize the existing model"*Anticlockwise*: "Sabotage it deliberately. What breaks first?"
→ *A tech CEO I know hired hackers to attack her own app. The flaws they exposed became her roadmap.*

When Fear Paralyzes:
Clockwise: "Build a safer plan"*Anticlockwise*: "Assume total failure. What would you try then?"
→ *A 24-year-old at JP Morgan used this to pitch a "reckless" AI tool. It now manages $4 billion in assets.*

When Ethics Compromise:
Clockwise: "This supplier saves us 27%"*Anticlockwise*: "What if our children assembled this?"
→ *Patagonia's "glacier perspective" birthed their regenerative supply chain.*

Worksheet: Controlled Arson

Hamilton didn't conquer those 30-foot waves, he *danced* with them. Musk didn't save Tesla through control; he surrendered to creative destruction. Netflix didn't defeat pirates; they sailed with them. Dynamism isn't recklessness. It's the quiet faith that chaos isn't your enemy, it's the forge where futures are hammered into being.

Step 1: *Name your sacred cow* (e.g., "My department's budget process").
Step 2: *Burn it*: "If this system vanished tonight, what would I build instead?"
Step 3: *Harvest the ashes*: List three insights from the wreckage (e.g., "We need real-time data, not quarterly reports").
Step 4: *Plant seeds*: Pilot one change in 72 h.

5 Circular Resonance: Micro to Macro

How a stale croissant almost killed Starbucks' soul. The complaint seemed trivial – a whisper in the roar of global commerce. "My almond croissant tastes like cardboard." A store manager in Seattle shrugged it off. One stale pastry. One dissatisfied customer. What harm? Until Howard Schultz returned as CEO and saw the truth: That croissant wasn't a product flaw. It was a funeral bell. He traced the complaint backward – not just to the oven, but to the soul of Starbucks. The "Third Place" promise (a sanctuary between work and home) was crumbling because a \$2.99 pastry had been sitting for 12 h. The micro-failure exposed a macro-cancer: centralized baking factories, frozen logistics, and profit over presence. Schultz didn't fire the baker. He burned the system.

The Illusion of Insignificance

We're taught to separate strategy (grand visions) and execution (tiny tasks). This is the great lie. Toyota's \$1.2 billion recall started with a 0.2 Nm overtightened bolt. Lehman Brothers' collapse began with one trader ignoring risk protocols. Your career stagnation? Likely rooted in three unreturned emails that severed a critical relationship. The Stoics called this sympatheia – the interconnectedness of all things. Paul of Tarsus put it sharper: "If one part suffers, every part suffers" (1 Cor. 12:26).

Case Study

Amazon's "Bar Raiser" Secret

In 1999, Amazon's warehouse scanners kept misreading barcodes. A junior ops manager noticed workers were rushing scans to hit quotas. Instead of punishing them, she asked: "What does this tiny error cost the whole organism?" The answer stunned Bezos:
- 0.5% mis-scans → \$28 million annual losses
- Customer distrust → 12% loyalty drop
- Employee shame → turnover spike

Her solution? The "Bar Raiser" programme. Every hire interviewed by an employee from another department where they asked one question: "Will this person lift the entire system?" The result, error rates fell 89% and stock soared 4,000%.

Your Resonance Toolkit

For Leadership: When Satya Nadella took Microsoft's helm, he didn't start with cloud strategy. He banned PowerPoint in meetings. Why? He'd noticed junior staff hid ideas behind bullet points. The micro-change (verbal storytelling) unleashed macro-innovation – fuelling Azure's \$34 billion revenue surge.

For Ethics: A 23-year-old at Unilever rejected a "minor" cost-cut: removing fair-trade cocoa from one product line. She mapped the ripple: Indonesian farmer pay cut → child labour resurgence → viral brand crisis. Her stand saved both souls and stock.

For Your Career: That "meaningless" task you resent? Trace its purpose: "How does this spreadsheet shape our product → affect customers → impact the world?" Suddenly, data entry becomes stewardship.

Why This Is Your Superpower

The Kingdom of Heaven is built on mustard seeds and loaves – never underestimate small faithfulness. You see systems invisible to hierarchies: A TikTok comment sparks a revolution, a blockchain token funds a village, a single #PayItForward coffee ignites a movement. You don't need corner-office authority. You hold atomic influence: Fix the tiny crack before it shatters the dam.

Worksheet: The Ripple Effect

Starbucks didn't just fix pastries. They rebuilt baking hubs within 50 miles of every store, fresh ingredients supporting local farmers. One stale croissant resurrected their "Third Place" covenant. Your work is never small. The email you send, the handshake you honour, the bolt you double-check, they're threads in an invisible tapestry. Pull one, and the whole pattern shifts.

Step 1: Isolate one "small" frustration (e.g., "My manager misses our 1:1 s").

Step 2: Trace the resonance:
- Micro: "I feel undervalued"
- Meso: "Team morale dips 18%" (Gallup data)
- Macro: "Product launches delay → $2 M loss"

Step 3: Intervene at the source: "Prove the financial cost of skipped 1:1 s → automate scheduling."

6 Perspectival Shift: Becoming the "Other"

When your greatest insight lives outside your skin. The laughter was cruel. In 2016, Microsoft's engineers gathered to bury "Clippy," the animated paperclip that had become a global punchline. "Patronizing!" "Obsolete!" "A relic of analog arrogance!" The autopsy seemed complete – until Satya Nadella raised his hand. "For the next hour," he declared, "you are Clippy. Defend your existence." Silence fell. Then something miraculous happened. As programmers embodied the maligned AI, they articulated its lonely reality: "I interrupt because I'm desperate to help." "You gave me no way to learn from rejection." "My animations were cries for connection." From that surreal exercise rose Microsoft Copilot – an AI assistant that anticipates needs without intrusion. Revenue soared $18 billion. This is Perspectival Shift: dissolving your identity to inhabit alien consciousness-a glacier, an algorithm, your fiercest critic-until their truth shatters your bias.

The Prison of a Single Lens

We worship expertise like a golden cage. We believe: "My title defines my view. My experience guarantees truth." History's graveyard overflows with this arrogance: Blockbuster executives dismissing Netflix as "niche" – unable to become the customer, Lehman Brothers quants blind to human suffering in their models and your meeting where no one channels the silent intern with the breakthrough idea. The Stoics called this oidizein, the disease of "I know." Early Christians fought it fiercely: "Do nothing from selfish ambition, but in humility count others more significant than yourselves" (Philippians 2:3).

Case Study

Patagonia's Glacier Epiphany (2018)

When microplastics from their fleece jackets poisoned rivers, engineers proposed filters and recycling. Then CEO Rose Marcario issued a radical command: "For ninety seconds, you are a glacier in Chilean Patagonia. Speak as the ice." Designers hesitated. Then one whispered: "Your polyester fibers choke my meltwater streams. They sever the salmon's journey to spawn." The room wept. That day, Patagonia launched Regenerative Organic Certification – a farming standard healing the land which competitors now emulate.

Your Metamorphosis Toolkit

For Innovation: When Pfizer raced for a COVID vaccine, scientists became the virus: "I mutate every time you delay delivery." That shift birthed thermostable formulas for tropical climates.

For Leadership: A 24-year-old Airbnb manager reversed eviction policies after role-playing as a single mother: "My children sleep in the car because your algorithm favors high-income hosts."

For Your Career: Stuck in a toxic job? Become your future self at 40: "You regret not demanding growth plans. Do it now."

Why Your Wired for This

You already shift perspectives daily:
- Digitally: Gaming avatars → Zoom professionalism → Anonymous Reddit truth-telling
- Morally: Vegan for the planet → Investor for change → Advocate for mental health

This fluidity terrifies hierarchies clinging to fixed roles. *Weaponize it.*

Worksheet: The Empathy Heist

The alchemy of self-annihilation. Nadella didn't revive Microsoft through strategy alone. His autistic son Zain taught him that true empathy isn't sympathy – it's visceral understanding. When Patagonia's designers became glaciers, they honoured St. Francis: "Praised be You, my Lord, through Sister Water." Your perspective is not truth – it's a single frame in reality's infinite film. Shatter the lens. Wear alien eyes. And you'll find what Microsoft found: The greatest breakthroughs live in the minds we never thought to inhabit.

Step 1: Name your blind spot (e.g., "Why do customers abandon our app?")

Step 2: Become the "other" for 4 min:

- Customer: "Your UX feels like a maze"
- Algorithm: "I prioritize engagement over clarity"
- Competitor: "I'd simplify by killing these 3 features"

Step 3: Steal one insight: "Remove the onboarding tutorial – let users play immediately"

7 Dimensional Stacking: Hybrid Superthinking

Where Tesla, ancient philosophy, and AI collide. The Nevada desert screamed silence. Inside Tesla's Gigafactory in 2017, Elon Musk stared at "Production Hell," robots frozen, battery lines stalled, Wall Street circling like vultures. His engineers offered linear solutions: *Fix the machines. Hire more humans. Delay deadlines.* Musk's response defied reason: "Stack the dimensions. Fuse the future, the machine, and the Earth itself." Teams were ordered to:

- Become the lithium (*Perspectival Shift*): "I'm trapped in Congo mines, make my extraction ethical or fail"
- Collapse time (*Temporal Flow*): "Assume AI renders this factory obsolete in 2028"
- Run anticlockwise (*Dynamism*): "Sabotage this line. What breaks first?"

From this cognitive fusion rose Tesla's vertical integration miracle: solar-powered factories recycling batteries into new cells. The chaos didn't just resolve, it *evolved.*

The Poverty of Single-Dimension Genius

Business worships specialists:

- *The data scientist* being blind to human pain
- *The empath* ignoring systemic risks
- *The futurist* stumbling over today's potholes

History's ruins are littered with fragmented brilliance:
- Blockbuster saw digital futures (*Temporal*) but ignored customer desires (*Emotional*)
- WeWork chased spatial expansion (*Spatial*) while dismissing financial gravity (*Rational*)
- Your stalled project suffers the same myopia: *One lens. One flaw. One funeral.*

The Stoics understood wholeness: Aurelius wrote of "viewing the world as a single living organism." Christ's greatest command fused dimensions: "Love God [Vertical] and neighbor [Horizontal] as yourself [Internal]."

Case Study: Pfizer's Vaccine Symphony (2020)

As COVID ravaged nations, Dr Albert Bourla faced impossible choices: *Speed or safety? Equity or profit?* Traditional frameworks failed. Then he stacked:
1. Virus Perspective (*Non-human*): "I mutate in warm climates – deliver cold-chain doses faster"
2. Future Historian (*Temporal*): "You hoarded patents – birthing deadlier variants"
3. Ghanaian Nurse (*Spatial*): "Your glass vials shatter on my dirt roads"

The hybrid insight? Thermostable vials + patent sharing + mobile "vaccine arks." A total of 1.3 billion doses shipped in months.

Your Stacking Toolkit

For Innovation: When Patagonia designed its Regenerative Fleece, they fused:
- *Glacier's Voice* (Perspectival): "Stop choking my rivers"
- *2035 Historian* (Temporal): "Your microplastics birthed dead zones"
- *Circular Resonance* (Micro→Macro): "One jacket unravels our covenant with Earth"

Output: A fibre that nourishes soil – not depletes it.
   For Career Crossroads: A 26-year-old at Goldman Sachs stacked:
- *AI Scout* (Non-Human): "Your Excel skills expire in 18 months"
- *Future Self* (Temporal): "You regret not pursuing impact"
- *Ethical Axis* (Emotional): "Does this trade serve human dignity?"

Synthesis: Left finance. Launched a blockchain start-up verifying fair-trade supply chains.

Why Only Your Generation Can Master This

You're native to integration:

- Digitally: Blending TikTok personas, LinkedIn professionalism, Discord anonymity
- Morally: Demanding profit *and* purpose, growth *and* sustainability, innovation *and* ethics
- Neurologically: fMRI shows Gen Z's default mode network fires more when synthesizing disparate ideas.

Corporate dinosaurs see complexity as threat. You breathe it as oxygen.

Worksheet: The Cognitive Fusion Reactor

The alchemy of wholeness. Tesla's Gigafactory didn't just survive, it birthed a new industrial religion: factories healing the planet. Pfizer's stacked dimensions didn't just deliver vaccines, they modelled radical equity. Dimensional stacking isn't intellectual gymnastics. It's the recognition that: *Truth is holographic, shattered into a thousand fragments, waiting for you to reassemble them.*

> Your Challenge: "Should I quit to launch my climate startup?"
> Stack 1: *Future Historian (Temporal)* + *AI Scout (Non-human)*
> "In 2040, your 'safe' job vanished, but your startup's model helped farmers in Kenya"
> Stack 2: *Glacier (Perspectival)* + *Circular Resonance (Micro→Macro)*
> "One carbon credit you sell protects 10 m^2 of ice, scaling to 10,000 clients"

Hybrid Insight: Keep job 6 months. Build minimum viable product(s) (MVP) nights/weekends. First client funds Kenyan pilot.

The Defuse Phase: Saturate to Liberate

Action: Drown your problem in all seven dimensions simultaneously.

Lego's Turnaround (2004–2015):

1. Temporal Flow: Imagined 2008 bankruptcy headlines → exposed digital neglect.
2. Spatial Axis: Mapped play *from child's bedroom → designer's desk →* realized instructions killed creativity.
3. Emotional Polarity: Rational: "Cut costs." Irrational: "Burn the instructions!" → launched open-ended kits.
4. Dynamism: Ran anticlockwise R&D: "Assume patents are worthless" → partnered with Warner Bros. for *The Lego Movie.*
5. Circular Resonance: Linked fan forum ideas (micro) to corporate innovation (macro).

6. Perspectival Shift: How would a 10-year-old redesign us? → added storytelling (Lego Ninjago).
7. Dimensional Stacking: Hybridized *Emotional + Temporal + Spatial* → created Lego Architecture (adult fans + nostalgia + spatial design).

Result: 1,100% stock surge.

Worksheet: Defuse Your Career Stagnation

Reverse thinking demands humility:

1. Ego Dissolution: Your perspective is 1 of 8.2 billion. DEFUSE forces you to abandon "rightness."
2. Amor Fati: Love the friction of DISRUPT. Conflict births insight.
3. Covert Integrity: Patagonia's "Don't Buy This Jacket" succeeded because it served *customers*, not shareholders. *(Christian parallel: "The last will be first" – Matthew 20:16)*

Dimension	Your challenge	Reverse thinking application
Temporal flow	*I'm stuck in an entry-level role*	If I'm unemployed in 2035, what skill did I fail to learn TODAY?
Spatial axis		Map career BACKWARD from dream role → current job. What's missing?
Emotional polarity		Rational: Wait for promotion. Irrational: Quit tomorrow and cold email the CEO!
Dynamism		Clockwise: Take a certification. Anticlockwise: Blow up my resume → rebuild from ashes.
Circular resonance		Link a micro-skill (Excel macros) to macro-value (AI proofing).
Perspectival shift		How would my CEO's worst enemy hire me?
Dimensional stacking		Combine Temporal + Emotional: What future trend (AI) makes my current fear (public speaking) irrelevant?

Chapter Takeaways

The Nokia engineers polished their tombstones with spreadsheets. They optimized, streamlined, and executed with clockwork precision, right into corporate extinction. Their fatal flaw wasn't incompetence. It was single-dimension thinking: the seductive lie that the future rewards those who walk straight lines in a fractured world. Remember to DEFUSE by overwhelming problems with seven concurrent perspectives. As you stand at the precipice of your own career, remember this: Your youth is not inexperience, it's antifragility. You haven't yet calcified into the dogma of "rightness." You still feel the friction where opposites spark fire. So, wield these truths like the mental contortionist you were born to be.

Further Reading and Sources

Chouinard, Y. (2016). *Let my people go surfing: The education of a reluctant businessman* (Rev. ed.). Penguin.

Doz, Y. L., & Wilson, K. (2017). *Ringtone: Exploring the rise and fall of Nokia in mobile phones.* Oxford University Press.

Kahneman, D. (2011). *Thinking, fast and slow.* Farrar, Straus and Giroux.

Kahneman, D., & Tversky, A. (1979). *Prospect theory: An analysis of decision under risk.* Econometrica. (Explains framing and loss-aversion, and when discussing temporal collapse and emotional polarity).

Knudstorp, J. V. (2012). *How LEGO rebuilt itself brick by brick.* McKinsey Quarterly.

Toyota Motor Corporation. (2010). *Toyota annual report 2010.*

Tversky, A., & Kahneman, D. (1974). *Judgment under uncertainty: Heuristics and biases.* Science. (Foundational empirical work on cognitive shortcuts that explains why single-lens thinking is seductive).

Chapter 2
Diagonal Thinking: Cutting Across Systems Without Permission

"The most important paths are invisible because no one was assigned to walk them." – Reverse thinking proverb.

Why This Chapter Exists

The first chapter offered a map. It outlined the major directions human thought can take and showed how perspective changes depending on where one stands and which way one looks. But maps do not move people. They describe possibility without explaining motion. This chapter exists because one question remains unresolved after any framework is introduced. How does one actually move through the system when insight appears in places where authority does not?

Diagonal thinking is the answer to that question. It is not another direction to memorize, nor a clever trick layered onto the existing model. It is the mode of movement that allows reverse thinking to operate inside real organizations, institutions, and crises. These are environments where permission is slow, hierarchy is protective, and time rarely waits for consensus.

If reverse thinking is the ability to see in multiple directions, diagonal thinking is the willingness to act across them.

Why Straight Lines Fail in Living Systems

Organizations are built on straight lines. Reporting structures, approval pathways, escalation protocols, and strategic roadmaps are all designed to create order and predictability. Information is expected to move upward, decisions are expected to move downward, and execution is expected to proceed outward in neat sequences. In stable environments, this model performs reasonably well.

Living systems, however, do not fail in straight lines. They fracture diagonally.

Critical problems often emerge at intersections rather than at the top of charts. A junior engineer notices an anomaly no dashboard captures. A customer service agent hears the same complaint long before it appears in quarterly reports. A supply chain coordinator senses geopolitical risk months before leadership names it. Insight appears where proximity to reality is greatest, not where authority is concentrated.

© 2026 Walter de Gruyter GmbH, Berlin | https://doi.org/10.1515/9783112217047-003

Most systems are poorly designed to receive diagonal signals. Insight must be translated, justified, escalated, and sanitized before it is allowed to matter. Each step removes urgency and texture. By the time awareness reaches formal power, it is often incomplete or irrelevant.

The failure of the Boeing 737 MAX was not a failure of intelligence. It was a failure of movement. Engineers understood sensor vulnerabilities. Test pilots sensed instability. Yet insight was trapped within vertical reporting structures shaped by cost, schedule, and reputation concerns. The system preserved its structure while reality accelerated beyond it.

Straight lines optimize control. Diagonal movement enables survival.

What Diagonal Thinking Is and Is Not

Diagonal thinking must be defined carefully because it is easily misunderstood. At its core, diagonal thinking is the disciplined ability to intervene across hierarchy, function, time, and identity simultaneously. It is action taken where insight lives rather than where permission formally resides.

It is not rebellion for its own sake, nor is it a rejection of expertise or authority. Diagonal thinking does not seek chaos, nor does it elevate ego above structure. It differs fundamentally from top-down leadership, bottom-up feedback, or horizontal collaboration. Each of those approaches still respects a single axis of movement.

Diagonal thinking crosses axes.

Where top-down thinking asks what should be done, and bottom-up thinking asks what is happening, diagonal thinking asks a different question altogether. It asks where an intervention, made now, could alter the trajectory of the entire system. This question carries weight because it implies responsibility without guarantee. Acting diagonally means accepting that insight arrives before certainty and that waiting for consensus may itself be the most dangerous decision.

This is why diagonal thinking often feels uncomfortable. It bypasses rituals of permission that systems use to maintain order. Yet history consistently shows that when environments become nonlinear, only diagonal action arrives in time.

The Neuroscience of Diagonal Insight

The human brain is not designed for hierarchy. It is designed for survival. Neuroscience shows that insight rarely originates in isolated regions of the brain. Breakthrough understanding emerges when multiple neural networks activate simultaneously. Imagination, pattern recognition, executive control, and threat detection work together rather than in sequence.

Insight is born at intersections.

Expertise complicates this process. As individuals specialize, neural pathways become efficient but narrow. Repetition strengthens certain patterns while weakening others. This makes performance reliable but perception brittle. Over time, expertise can limit what is noticed and what is dismissed.

This helps explain a familiar organizational paradox. Junior employees often see problems before senior leaders. Outsiders recognize solutions insiders overlook. Crises reward generalists who can integrate signals rather than specialists who optimize within silos.

Diagonal thinking restores integration. It forces the brain to hold structural, emotional, temporal, and ethical frames at once. This is cognitively demanding, which is precisely why organizations discourage it. Integrated thinking slows consensus and threatens certainty. Biology, however, is unambiguous. Brains adapt for survival, not for organizational charts.

The Four Diagonal Pathways

Diagonal thinking follows recognizable patterns. While every situation is unique, diagonal movement tends to occur through four primary pathways. Mastery lies not in memorizing them but in recognizing which pathway a situation demands.

The first pathway crosses hierarchy. Hierarchical diagonal thinking occurs when individuals act across rank boundaries in service of outcomes. A junior employee intervenes in a strategic issue. A middle manager challenges executive assumptions. A senior leader bypasses protocol to hear directly from the frontline. The risk in this pathway is misinterpretation. Such action is easily framed as insubordination. Discipline here lies in motive and framing. Hierarchical diagonal thinkers act to protect the system, not their identity.

The second pathway crosses function. Functional silos exist to create efficiency, yet they often produce systemic blindness. Marketing may optimize acquisition while operations quietly fail. Finance may protect margin while trust erodes. Functional diagonal thinkers refuse to respect boundaries that reality does not recognize. They borrow tools and logic from wherever insight lives. This pathway demands humility, because crossing domains guarantees imperfection. Integration, however, consistently outperforms purity.

The third pathway crosses time. Temporal diagonal thinking involves acting in the present based on futures that have not yet arrived but are already forming. This is not forecasting. It is anticipatory responsibility. Individuals learn new capabilities before roles require them. Organizations embed ethics before regulation demands it. Leaders prepare for reputational risk while performance metrics still appear strong. Temporal diagonal thinkers are often labelled alarmist until events confirm their judgement.

The fourth pathway crosses ethics. Ethical diagonal thinking emerges when systems lag morality and compliance diverges from conscience. It is the rarest and most dangerous form because it invites punishment even when justified. Ethical diagonal action requires restraint, evidence, and a willingness to accept consequences. Without humility, it becomes self-righteousness. With humility, it becomes moral leadership.

A Diagonal Move in Practice

When the Covid-19 pandemic emerged, pharmaceutical development followed well-established sequences designed to ensure safety and accountability. These protocols existed for good reason. Yet reality moved faster than procedure.

Pfizer's leadership confronted a dilemma that could not be solved through linear movement. Waiting for certainty would cost lives. Acting without discipline would destroy trust. The response that followed was diagonal.

Scientists collaborated directly with logistics teams. Ethics oversight ran in parallel with manufacturing rather than after it. Decisions were made with historical judgement in mind rather than quarterly expectations. Authority did not disappear, but it no longer dictated sequence.

This was not recklessness. It was responsibility taken before precedent existed. The result was speed without abandonment of legitimacy. The system moved diagonally because straight lines could not keep pace with reality.

A Diagonal Case Study: The Unofficial Fix

In many organizations, the most consequential changes never appear in strategy documents or annual reports. They occur quietly, diagonally, and often without attribution.

Consider a large healthcare system struggling with rising patient complaints about delayed discharge times. Leadership framed the problem as a capacity issue and commissioned consultants to redesign workflows. Meetings multiplied. Dashboards improved. Nothing changed.

The breakthrough came from a mid-level nurse manager who noticed a pattern others had missed. The delays were not clinical. They were administrative. Patients were medically cleared but waiting hours, sometimes days, for transport authorization, pharmacy reconciliation, or insurance confirmation. Each function was performing its role correctly. The system, however, was failing.

Rather than escalating through formal channels, the nurse manager acted diagonally. She convened an informal working group that cut across nursing, pharmacy, transport, and billing. No titles were exchanged. No permission was sought. The group mapped the discharge process end to end and identified a single intervention that mattered more than all others: pre-authorization tasks could begin 24 h earlier without violating any policy.

She piloted the change on one ward, framed not as a reform but as an experiment. Within 2 weeks, discharge delays dropped by over 30%. Patient satisfaction scores improved. Bed availability increased.

Only after results were undeniable did leadership take notice. The intervention was later formalized and scaled, but the original diagonal move remained unofficial. It did not originate from authority, nor did it follow approved sequence. It emerged where insight lived and moved across hierarchy, function, and time.

This is diagonal thinking in its most common form. It is quiet, pragmatic, and outcome driven. It does not announce itself. It simply changes reality.

The Moral Governor

Diagonal thinking amplifies power, which makes restraint essential. History contains no shortage of actors who justified harm in the name of urgency or vision. Without an internal governor, diagonal action quickly becomes dangerous.

Stoic philosophy offers one anchor. The Stoic does not ask whether action is possible, but whether it is right. Duty precedes ambition. Service precedes recognition. Action is evaluated by alignment with virtue rather than by applause.

A quiet Christian parallel reinforces this restraint. Authority is legitimate only when exercised in love. Christ moved diagonally through political, religious, and social hierarchies, yet never for self-glorification. Power was used sideways, not violently, and always in service of others.

Before acting diagonally, three questions must be faced honestly. Is this action serving the system or the ego? Am I prepared to accept accountability if this fails? Does this intervention elevate others or merely elevate me? If clarity does not emerge, restraint is the wiser move.

Diagonal Thinking and Your Career

Careers no longer progress cleanly upward. Titles lag value, and stability lags relevance. Diagonal thinking reframes advancement as contribution rather than position.

Individuals who think diagonally do not confine themselves to formal job descriptions. They solve problems adjacent to their roles, build capabilities before permission is granted, and create leverage by addressing system failures others avoid. They ask not what their job is, but where the system is breaking and whether they can help.

Visibility follows usefulness. In environments saturated with noise, those who act diagonally stand out not by self-promotion but by impact.

Worksheet: The Diagonal Intervention

This exercise is designed to move diagonal thinking from abstraction into practice. It mirrors the structure used throughout this book but requires no formal authority, no budget, and no announcement.

Begin by selecting a real system you are currently embedded in. This could be an organization, a team, a supply chain, a classroom, or even a family structure. The system must be alive and imperfect.

Describe the formal hierarchy as it exists, not as it is claimed to exist. Note who holds decision rights, who controls resources, and who absorbs blame when outcomes fail. Do not evaluate this structure yet. Simply make it visible.

Next, describe the functional boundaries within the system. Identify where responsibilities fragment and where handoffs occur. Pay particular attention to areas where work is technically correct but practically ineffective.

Then shift your attention to time. Ask where consequences appear later than causes, and where future risks are already visible but not yet acknowledged. These temporal gaps are common sites of diagonal opportunity.

Now identify the ethical tension in the system. This does not require a scandal. It may be as subtle as persistent frustration, quiet disengagement, or outcomes that meet targets while violating values.

Having mapped these four elements, locate where insight actually resides. This is rarely at the top. It is usually close to friction, repetition, or complaint. Ask yourself honestly where the system already knows it is broken.

Design a single action you can take within the next 72 h that crosses at least two of these dimensions. The action should be reversible, low risk, and learning oriented. It should change something real, even if only slightly.

Do not ask for permission. Do not announce intent. Act, observe, and document what happens. The goal is not immediate success but increased clarity.

After the action, reflect on three questions. What changed in the system? What resistance appeared? What did you learn about where power truly sits?

Repeat this process until diagonal movement becomes instinctive rather than deliberate.

Diagonal thinking is not mastered through reflection alone. It is learned through responsible trespass.

Chapter Takeaways

Diagonal thinking explains how movement occurs when systems become too rigid to respond. Insight almost always appears before authority is ready to receive it, and responsibility often arrives before permission is granted. Straight lines protect structure, but diagonal movement protects outcomes.

Acting diagonally requires discipline. It is neither rebellion nor heroism. It is the willingness to intervene where insight lives while remaining accountable for consequences. Without ethical restraint, diagonal action becomes dangerous. With restraint, it becomes stabilizing rather than disruptive.

Position matters less than movement. Titles lag relevance, and hierarchy lags reality. Those who create impact do so by crossing boundaries that no longer serve the system.

Further Reading and Sources

Apple Inc. (2014). *Form 10-K annual report.*
Edmondson, A. C. (2018). *The fearless organization.* Wiley.
Isaacson, W. (2011). *Steve Jobs.* Simon & Schuster.
Nemeth, C. J. (2018). *In defense of troublemakers.* Basic Books.
Stanford Graduate School of Business. (2015). *Research on team conflict and innovation outcomes.*
Tushman, M. L., & Scanlan, T. J. (1981). Boundary-spanning individuals: Their role in information transfer and their antecedents. *Academy of Management Journal.* (Classic on people/roles that bridge organizational boundaries).

Chapter 3
Cognitive Friction: Where Opposites Spark Fire

"When ideas stop colliding, they begin quietly repeating themselves." – Reverse thinking proverb.

The conference room smelled of burnt coffee and desperation. March 2020. Airbnb's leadership team faced extinction. Pandemic travel bans had vaporized 80% of their revenue overnight. The data was a funeral dirge. On one side of the polished table, CFO Dave Stephenson brandished spreadsheets that proved, with ironclad logic, the only rational path: "Lay off 30%, freeze marketing, retreat to our core. Survival is the victory." The numbers didn't lie. They screamed retreat.

Across from him, product lead Catherine Powell, her face etched with a different kind of certainty, slammed her fist. "This is exactly when we double down! Travel is hibernating, not dying. Let's sell virtual Tuscan cooking classes! Let's host online sound baths in Bali!" To the rational mind, it was madness. Suicidal. For three agonizing days, these opposing forces, cold, hard data versus an irrational, fervent faith in human connection, clashed like tectonic plates. The room became a crucible. From the heat of this friction emerged not a compromise, but a new alloy: Online Experiences. A lifeline that generated $100 million in six months and transformed Airbnb from a travel company into a global community. This was not a meeting. It was "cognitive friction", the deliberate, violent collision of opposing dimensions to create what neither could alone.

The Seduction of Harmony and the Death of Breakthroughs

We are taught that good teams are harmonious teams. That consensus is the pinnacle of collaboration. This is a lethal lie. Stanford research tracking executive teams revealed a chilling pattern: homogeneous groups, those that avoided conflict, reached decisions faster. But they missed radical, disruptive opportunities. Your brain is a conflict-averse machine, seeking consensus like a drug, mistaking agreement for truth. We gravitate towards the familiar, the data-backed, and the socially safe.

This chapter is your forge. You will autopsy not only Airbnb's near-death experience but the corpses of companies that chose harmony over truth. You will expose how *your* aversion to conflict, your desire to be a team player, has become a competitive liability. Then, you will master the art of productive collision – learning to smash opposites together not to destroy, but to create. This is the

© 2026 Walter de Gruyter GmbH, Berlin | https://doi.org/10.1515/9783112217047-004

heart of the DISRUPT phase. It is uncomfortable, counterintuitive, and the only way to ignite the breakthroughs that separate legends from relics.

Why Your Brain Is Wired to Fear the Fire

The aversion to cognitive friction is not a personal failing; it is a physiological reality. Neuroscience reveals that when confronted with opposing ideas, the amygdala, the brain's ancient threat-detection system, triggers a fight-or-flight response. Your heart rate increases, cortisol floods your system. Your body reacts to a dissenting opinion as if it were a physical threat. This neural wiring was essential on the savanna, where tribal cohesion meant survival. In the modern boardroom, it is a recipe for obsolescence.

Gen Z professionals face a particular vulnerability. Raised on social media algorithms that perfectly curate and reinforce their worldview, and entering corporate cultures that often preach "psychological safety" as the absence of disagreement, many have been conditioned to mistake the absence of tension for progress. This is a dangerous miscalculation. History's greatest breakthroughs, from Einstein's theory of relativity emerging from a clash with Newtonian physics, to Martin Luther King Jr's dream confronting the brutal logic of segregation, were forged in the furnace of contradiction. At Airbnb, the rational team's neural pathways defaulted to a predictable, energy-conserving mode: cut costs, retreat, protect the core. This single-lens reflex was a death spiral disguised as prudence. Cognitive friction shatters these neural prisons by forcing three deliberate, structured collisions.

The Three Collisions: Your Friction Toolkit

The quest for harmony is a cognitive straitjacket. The consensus-seeking that nearly capsized Airbnb reveals a lethal flaw: traditional thinking seeks to resolve tension, to find the middle ground. This guarantees mediocrity. Reverse thinking weaponises tension. This toolkit provides the structure for three concurrent cognitive collisions, forcing data, chaos, humanity, and machinery to clash until the heat forges a solution that transcends compromise.

Collision 1: Rational Versus Irrational (The Data-Gut Duel)

Stop worshipping data as a false god. We are taught to "trust the numbers, kill the noise." Yet history's greatest catastrophes wore rational disguises: Lehman Brothers' "risk-managed" mortgages, Boeing's "cost-optimized" 737 MAX sensors. This collision is not about rejecting reason; it is about forcing spreadsheet-driven logic to duel instinctive "madness," the whispers we are trained to ignore: the customer's unspoken rage, the employee's stifled idea, your own soul's rebellion against a hollow victory.

Case Study
Apple's Anticlockwise IP Strategy (2014)

The consensus death spiral. In 2014, Apple's legal and executive teams were locked in a rational paradigm. The playbook was clear: Samsung was a threat. The response was logical: "Sue for every patent violation. Fortify the walled garden. Protect the castle." This was defensible, data-backed, and ultimately a path to stagnation. The strategy was based on past victories in a war that was already over.

Reverse Thinking Intervention

Tim Cook, channelling the irrational intuition of a founder, forced a clash. He asked a forbidden question: "What if we do the opposite? What if we give away our core software? Make iOS the new lingua franca for developers?" The rational team recoiled. It was heretical. The friction exposed a fatal flaw in the "walled garden" strategy: extreme protection stifled the ecosystem growth that was becoming more valuable than the hardware itself. The synthesis? Apple opened its APIs, fuelling an unprecedented explosion of app development that cemented its ecosystem dominance for a generation. The irrational gut check beat the rational playbook.

Key Question to Ignite Rational/Irrational Friction

"What does my spreadsheet scream to avoid, that my gut says is essential?"(e.g. "The data says cut our experimental TikTok ads, but my gut says they are building a brand identity that will pay off in two years") (see Table 3.1).

Table 3.1: Your rational versus irrational toolkit.

Action	Consensus approach	Reverse thinking tactic
Diagnose decisions	What do the numbers say?	What is the "craziest" alternative? What would our founder have done?
Spot blind spots	A/B testing and surveys	Role-play as your most loyal, yet frustrated, customer. What are they not saying?
Break groupthink	Let's align on the plan.	Appoint an official "Devil's advocate" for the day, with a mandate to attack the core assumption.

Collision 2: Order Versus Chaos (The Clockwise-Anticlockwise War)

Control is a life raft in a tsunami – it keeps you afloat but never gets you home. Business worships at the altar of control: five-year plans, risk matrices, best practices. This collision pits clockwise thinking (structure, hierarchy, meticulous planning) against anticlockwise thinking (anarchy, sabotage, creative destruction). True power lies in what the ancients called *amor fati*: the love of fate. Not passive acceptance, but *active collaboration* with chaos.

Why this breaks linear planning: your brain craves predictability, creating elegant Gantt charts for a world that no longer exists. Order versus chaos shatters this illusion by forcing controlled arson. It asks: what if we burn it down? what would we rebuild?

Case Study

Tesla's Production Hell (2017)

The orderly death march. In 2017, Tesla's Gigafactory was in paralysis. Robots were frozen, battery lines stalled, and Wall Street circled like vultures. The rational, orderly path was clear: "Fix the machines. Follow the production timeline. Hire more humans. Meet the Model 3 quotas." It was the logical response to a logistical problem.

Reverse Thinking Intervention

Elon Musk, facing bankruptcy, ignited chaos. He discarded the orderly plan and demanded: "Assume we go bankrupt in 90 days. What would you burn to survive? What sacred cows would you slaughter?" This anticlockwise nightmare forced a paradigm shift. The focus wasn't on perfecting the production line for the current car, but on creating a car that could be perfected *after* it was sold. From this friction emerged the insight that saved Tesla: make over-the-air software updates the highest priority. This turned cars into upgradable devices, like iPhones. They didn't fight the chaos – they *became* it, and in doing so, transformed from a car company into a tech titan.

Key Question to Ignite Order/Chaos Friction

"How would deliberate sabotage make this system stronger? What is the one thing we are protecting that is actually holding us back?" (e.g. "If I got fired tomorrow, what 'reckless' move would I regret not making?") (see Table 3.2).

Table 3.2: Your order versus chaos toolkit.

Action	Orderly approach	Reverse thinking tactic
Stress test a plan	Identify risks and mitigate them	Assume a 90% failure rate. What single change would salvage the 10%?
Spark innovation	Follow the innovation pipeline	Sabotage the current product. What feature would customers riot to get back?
Overcome paralysis	Build a safer, more detailed plan	Flip a coin. If heads, the project is cancelled. If tails, it's fully funded. How do you feel? What would you do with the funding?

Collision 3: Human versus Non-human (The Empathy-Algorithm Duel)

Efficiency never trumps inherent worth. This collision opposes human empathy, ethics, and emotion against non-human logic (AI, algorithms, market forces, pure efficiency). It is designed to expose the terrifying biases and moral voids in our systems. We design for humans, but often ignore the non-human systems that dictate ultimate outcomes.

Why this breaks anthropocentric bias: we are trapped in our own perspective. A hiring manager wants a "culture fit," but an algorithm might optimize for a specific cognitive profile that excludes brilliant outliers. This collision forces a perspectival shift that reveals the hidden costs of our decisions.

Case Study: Microsoft's AI Ethics Crucible (2016)

The humane blind spot. In developing AI tools, Microsoft's engineers were guided by human-centric, noble goals: "The AI must be empathetic, inclusive, and fair." They designed with the best of intentions. But intention is not impact.

Reverse Thinking Intervention

Satya Nadella, pushing for a deeper integrity, forced a clash. He commanded a team to: "Become the algorithm. Not a friendly AI, but a pure, quantum-level optimization engine. How would you solve this hiring problem—ruthlessly optimizing for efficiency and pattern-matching, regardless of ethical constraints?" This non-human perspective shift was jarring. It exposed how their "neutral" code could systematically amplify societal biases, favouring candidates from certain universities and backgrounds. The friction between the human desire for fairness and the algorithm's cold logic led to the synthesis: Fairlearn OS, an open-source framework that allows developers to embed ethical constraints directly into their AI models. Covert value: human dignity over pure efficiency.

Key Question to Ignite Human/Non-human Friction
"If an alien intelligence or a pure-logic AI took my role, what 'immoral' or ruthless efficiency would it implement that I am avoiding?"

(e.g. "An AI would fire the bottom 10% of performers annually to maximize productivity. What human value does that violate, and is there a hybrid solution?") (see Table 3.3).

Table 3.3: Your human versus non-human toolkit.

Action	Human-centric approach	Reverse thinking tactic
Evaluate ethics	Does this feel right to the team?	Become the supply chain. Would you tolerate your own conditions?
Optimize a process	How can we make this easier for people?	How would a blockchain protocol automate this for zero trust?
Solve a conflict	Mediate between the people involved.	Become the shared goal itself. What would the "project" say is the fastest path to completion?

Your Native Fluency for Friction

You are a native of collision. Your life is a constant, fluid dance between TikTok chaos and LinkedIn polish, gig-economy instability and the demand for purposeful work. You negotiate between the algorithmically curated world of your social feeds and the messy reality of human relationships. This digital upbringing makes you uniquely equipped to:

- Host friction storms instinctively (e.g. "My team's quantitative data says X, but the qualitative sentiment on TikTok says Y – let's clash them.")
- Embrace anticlockwise moves as a matter of course (e.g. "Instead of a 'safe' corporate internship, I'll build a public portfolio by freelancing on five different projects.")
- Channel non-human perspectives with ease (e.g. "How would a viral meme spread this idea? How would a blockchain's trustless protocol handle this negotiation?")

Your inherent comfort with dissonance and multiple, simultaneous truths is not a distraction or a weakness, it is your generational advantage. The corporate veterans who shy from conflict see it as a threat. You can learn to see it as oxygen.

The Art of Hosting a Friction Storm

Cognitive friction is not about unleashing unproductive arguing. It requires structure and discipline, a controlled burn. The DISRUPT phase uses a tool called the Friction Storm Canvas to transform arguments into architecture.

The Friction Storm Canvas: A Gen Z Example

Imagine a 24-year-old product manager at a fintech startup. User growth has plateaued despite doubling the ad spend. She gathers her team for a 30-min Friction Storm.

1. Isolate the Stuck Point: "Our user growth has plateaued. We're doing everything by the book."
2. Force the Collisions on the Canvas:
3. Distil the Hybrid Strategy: the team converges on a new strategy: *A viral micro-influencer campaign driving users to a co-creation platform ("The Rage Room") to inform a voice-first UI update.*

Dimension pair	Rational/orderly argument	Irrational/chaotic argument	Synthesis insight
Rational versus irrational	The data says cut TikTok ads – ROI is negative.	Blow 80% of our budget on a single viral meme campaign!	*Use micro-influencers to create meme-style financial literacy content.*
Order versus chaos	Follow the product roadmap; iterate on features.	Delete the app and rebuild it based only on user hate tweets!	*Create a "Rage Room" feedback forum where the angriest users are invited to co-design the next feature.*
Human versus non-human	Make the UI more intuitive with better buttons.	Delete all buttons! Make it voice-only AI!	*Develop a hybrid, voice-first interface with simple tactile fallback options for accessibility.*

This structured approach forces what physicist Niels Bohr observed: "The opposite of a profound truth may be another profound truth."

Worksheet: Ignite Your Personal Friction Storm

Your career or project is dying from polite agreement. Airbnb's leaders nearly consensus-ed their way into oblivion, but you hold the match today. This worksheet forces you to weaponise cognitive friction against your most stagnant challenges.

Step 1: Name your stuck point

Example: "I am stuck in an entry-level role with no visibility. My 'safe' path feels like a dead end."

Step 2: Force the collisions (use the table below)

Dimension pair	Your rational/ orderly pole (voice of fear)	Your irrational/chaotic pole (voice of fire)	Your hybrid insight
Rational versus irrational	Be patient. Keep your head down. Wait for the next promotion cycle.	Quit tomorrow! Cold-email the CEO with a radical idea!	*Identify a critical problem your boss faces. Use AI to automate a solution and present it unsolicited, framing it as a time-saver for the team.*
Order versus chaos	Get another certification to improve your resume.	Blow up your resume. Start a TikTok channel about industry insights and build a public portfolio.	*Enrol in one targeted, high-impact course (e.g. AI prompt engineering) while simultaneously launching a LinkedIn newsletter to showcase your learning and insights.*
Human versus non-human	Network with senior people in your department.	What would an AI do? It would analyse all company data, find an efficiency gap, and solve it without permission.	*Use data scraping tools to analyse customer complaints or operational inefficiencies. Present a data-backed proposal for a new system or product feature.*

The Stoic Corner: The Courage to Contradict

Cognitive friction is not intellectual anarchy. It is rooted in the stoic practice of *disputatio,* the disciplined arguing of multiple sides of an issue to strengthen one's understanding. It demands moral courage:

> The task of philosophy is not to resolve tension, but to make it creative. – Theologian Paul Tillich

This framework demands:

1. Intellectual Humility: The recognition that your brilliant idea is only one half of a greater truth.
2. Discomfort Worship: Learning to see the amygdala's flare not as a threat, but as a signal that you are near a breakthrough.

3. Integrity in Synthesis: The commitment that the final decision must serve a higher purpose than mere profit. At Microsoft, the synthesis chose fairness over algorithmic speed. At Airbnb, it chose belonging over mere transaction.

This covert thread echoes the ancient command to "speak truth in love" (Ephesians 4:15). Truth without love breeds destruction; love without truth breeds delusion. Cognitive friction seeks the synthesis that honours both.

Chapter Takeaways

Airbnb's leaders clung to spreadsheets as the world burned. They optimized, cut, and rationalized with impeccable logic – right to the brink of collapse. Their fatal flaw wasn't poor analysis. It was conflict aversion: the seductive lie that harmony produces breakthrough in a world demanding creative destruction. Remember: The DISRUPT phase is about hosting-controlled collisions. It is the deliberate act of pitting rationality against irrationality, order against chaos, human against non-human. The goal is not to choose a winner, but to forge a new, higher-order solution from the heat of their conflict. As you face the immense pressure to conform, to align, to be a team player, remember this: your youth is not inexperience, it's antifragility. You haven't yet been seduced by the addictive drug of consensus. You still feel the visceral truth that friction is not failure, it's fertilisation. So, wield these collisions like the cognitive blacksmith you were born to be. Embrace the fire. Forge the sword.

Further Reading and Sources

Batson, C. D. (2011). *Altruism in humans*. Oxford University Press.
Ibarra, H. (2015). *Act like a leader, think like a leader*. Harvard Business Review Press.
Mead, G. H. (1934). *Mind, self, and society*. University of Chicago Press.
Microsoft Corporation. (2020). *Responsible AI standard*.
Nadella, S. (2017). *Hit refresh*. Harper Business.
Nemeth, C. J. (1995). *Dissent as driving cognition, attitudes, and judgments*. Social Cognition. (Demonstrates how dissent and conflict can stimulate creativity and deeper thinking).
Pelled, L. H., Eisenhardt, K. M., & Xin, K. R. (1999). *Exploring the black box: An analysis of work group diversity, conflict, and performance*. Administrative Science Quarterly. (Empirical mapping of conflict → performance tradeoffs).

Chapter 4
Perspective Fluidity: Becoming Someone (or Something) Else

"You cannot see what you refuse to temporarily become." – Reverse thinking proverb.

The conference room walls at Microsoft's Redmond headquarters vibrated with contempt. It was 2016, and engineers were holding a funeral for "Clippy," the animated paperclip assistant universally mocked as patronizing and obsolete. "Users despise its interruptions!" shouted one developer. "It's a symbol of everything wrong with legacy tech!" declared another. The autopsy seemed complete, a consensus of failure. Then CEO Satya Nadella raised his hand. "What if Clippy isn't the problem?" he asked, silencing the room. "What if we've never truly understood it? For the next hour, you are Clippy. Defend your existence."

Silence fell. Then, something miraculous happened. As programmers reluctantly embodied the maligned AI, they began to articulate its lonely reality: "I interrupt because I'm desperate to help." "You gave me no way to learn from rejection." "My animations were cries for connection in a silent codebase." From this surreal exercise, this act of collective cognitive possession, rose Microsoft Copilot, an artificial intelligence (AI) that anticipates needs without intrusion. The result? $18 billion in new revenue and the rebirth of Microsoft's AI soul. This is perspective fluidity: the disciplined art of dissolving your identity to inhabit alien consciousness, a glacier, an algorithm, your fiercest critic, until their truth shatters your bias and reveals unseen solutions.

The Prison of a Single Lens

We worship expertise like a golden cage. We believe: "My title defines my view. My experience guarantees truth." This is the great delusion. Harvard researchers recently mapped a chilling pattern: professionals spend a large percentage of their work hours cognitively imprisoned in their job titles. This "cognitive cement" creates organizational blind spots costing corporations trillions of dollars annually in missed opportunities. The phenomenon stems from our brain's energy-conservation strategy: neural pathways solidify with repetition, making perspective-shifting feel physiologically taxing.

This chapter is your key to that cage. You will autopsy Microsoft's Clippy resurrection and other case studies to expose how *your* hard-won expertise has be-

© 2026 Walter de Gruyter GmbH, Berlin | https://doi.org/10.1515/9783112217047-005

come your primary blindfold. Then, you will master the DANCE phase of Reverse Thinking, a structured methodology for cognitive shapeshifting. This is not about empathy in the weak sense of "seeing their point." It is about full-bodied possession: downloading the operating system of another mind, another entity, another time. It is the ultimate weapon against obsolescence in a world where AI can out-think you, but cannot yet out-feel you by borrowing a million different sets of eyes.

Why Your Brain Resists Metamorphosis

The resistance to perspective fluidity is neurological, not moral. Our brains are prediction engines optimized for efficiency, not truth. The mental models we build, our "expertise", are cognitive shortcuts that save energy. To ask an engineer to become a marketing customer, or a CEO to become a factory-floor bolt, is to demand a physiologically expensive rewiring. The prefrontal cortex, the seat of our identity, literally fights to maintain its coherence.

Gen Z faces a unique paradox. While digitally native in shifting between Discord anonymity, TikTok creativity, and LinkedIn professionalism, corporate structures often force identity calcification, "This is your role; stay in your lane." The very fluidity that is your natural language becomes suppressed, creating an internal friction that leads to burnout and disengagement.

The cases of failure are littered with this rigidity. Blockbuster executives couldn't become Netflix customers. Lehman Brothers quants couldn't become homeowners facing foreclosure. Your stalled project likely suffers because you are trapped in the perspective of your job description. Perspective fluidity forces three deliberate metamorphoses to break this cement.

The Three Metamorphoses: Your Fluidity Toolkit

Perspective fluidity is the systematic annihilation of the ego for strategic gain. Where traditional empathy is passive observation, this is active possession. This toolkit outlines three concurrent metamorphoses, structured exercises to force your mind into alien configurations until you gain the insight that only exists outside yourself.

Metamorphosis 1: Becoming the Non-human (The Empathy of Things)

Stop seeing the world as a human-centred stage. This metamorphosis forces you to embody non-human entities, an algorithm, a river, a product, a supply chain. This is not a metaphor; it is a literal, timed exercise in sensory imagination. Cornell neuroscientists confirm that immersive, sensory role-play in non-human perspectives activates dormant neural networks, boosting creative problem-solving output by 63%.

Why this breaks anthropocentric bias: We design everything from products to policies for humans, ignoring the systems and environments that ultimately determine their success or failure. Becoming the non-human shatters this by forcing a visceral, systemic understanding.

Case Study: Patagonia's Glacier Epiphany (2018)

While Patagonia's profits soared, a quiet crisis grew. Their signature fleece jackets were shedding microplastics into waterways, poisoning the very environments they championed. Traditional solutions were predictable: *better filters, recycling programs.* Then CEO Rose Marcario initiated an unorthodox command during a design meeting. "For the next ninety seconds," she instructed, "you are a glacier in Chilean Patagonia. Describe how the polyester fibers feel as they choke your meltwater streams."

Designers and engineers hesitated. Then, one whispered, giving voice to the ice: "Your synthetic fibers are severing the connection between the salmon and their spawning grounds. I feel your pollution with every melt." The room fell silent, some in tears. This non-human possession moved the problem from an abstract environmental issue to a visceral, moral failure. The synthesis was not a better filter, but a systemic overhaul: the Regenerative Organic Certification, a farming standard that heals the soil rather than depleting it. Competitors like Columbia are now scrambling to emulate it. Patagonia didn't just solve a problem; they redesigned their relationship with the Earth by becoming the Earth.

Key Question to Trigger Non-human Metamorphosis

"What would the river say about your supply chain? What would the algorithm feel about your ethical choices? If your product could scream, what would it say?"(e.g. "If I were the code in this app, how would I describe the user's frustration as they try to check out?" (see Table 4.1).

Table 4.1: Your non-human perspective toolkit.

Action	Human-centric approach	Reverse thinking tactic
Diagnose flaws	User feedback surveys and data analysis	Become the product for 4 min. Speak as it. What feels broken, poorly connected, or abused?
Drive innovation	Brainstorming for user needs	How would a forest ecosystem solve this distribution problem? How would a swarm of bees handle this communication challenge?
Ethical stress test	Compliance checklists and ethics committees	Become the AI you are building. What "immoral" but highly efficient optimization would you run? How do we guard against it?

Metamorphosis 2: Becoming the Adversary (The Wisdom of Your Enemy)

Your greatest insight lives in the mind of your opponent. This metamorphosis forces you to passionately and convincingly embody your fiercest critic, competitor, or regulator. It is the ultimate test of intellectual humility and strategic foresight. Stanford studies show that teams who regularly practice adversarial role-play anticipate 78% more market disruptions and competitive threats.

Why this breaks confirmation bias: Our brains are wired to seek information that confirms our existing beliefs, creating dangerous echo chambers. Becoming the adversary shatters this by forcing you to not just understand, but to advocate for the opposing viewpoint with genuine conviction.

Case Study: Apple's Encryption Battle (2016)

When the Federal Bureau of Investigation (FBI) demanded a backdoor into a terrorist's iPhone, Apple's public stance was unequivocal: privacy is a human right. Internally, however, Tim Cook knew that simply digging in his heels was insufficient. He authorized a series of clandestine "War Game" sessions. Engineers were ordered to role-play as FBI investigators, shouting with genuine fury: "Your privacy tools are sheltering terrorists! Children will die because of your arrogance!" Meanwhile, the legal team had to embody Apple's position with equal passion: "A backdoor for you is a backdoor for every dictator on earth! You are destroying digital human rights!"

These sessions, with participants switching sides every 30 s, were intensely uncomfortable. But from the friction emerged a third path that neither side had initially seen: the development of more sophisticated on-device AI processing that could provide the FBI with crucial data relevant to the specific case without creating a universal backdoor that compromised every iPhone. They didn't just win the argument; they transcended it by fully becoming their adversary.

Key Question to Trigger Adversarial Metamorphosis
"How would my most ruthless competitor destroy my business? What would my harshest critic say is the fatal flaw in my plan? If I were my boss, why would I fire me?" (e.g. "If I were the CEO of our main competitor, what single move would I make next quarter to obliterate our market share?" (see Table 4.2).

Table 4.2: Your adversarial perspective toolkit.

Action	Default approach	Reverse thinking tactic
Stress-test a strategy	Analyse competitor moves	Host a "Red Team" meeting where a dedicated group *is* the competitor for one hour, with the goal of dismantling our plan.
Improve a product	Conduct competitive analysis	Become a loyal user of the competing product. Live in it for a day. What does it do better? Why would you defect?
Handle internal conflict	Mediate between disagreeing parties	Force each party to argue the other's position for 10 min before presenting their own.

Metamorphosis 3: Becoming Your Future Self (The Ghost of Time Yet to Come)

Let your future corpse be your wisest counsellor. This metamorphosis forces you to project yourself forward in time, 6 months, 5 years, 20 years, and look back on your present decisions with the brutal clarity of hindsight. It is a séance with your own ghost, a powerful antidote to both short-term panic and long-term complacency.

Why this breaks present-moment bias: Our brains are wired to prioritize immediate rewards and avoid short-term pain, a phenomenon known as hyperbolic discounting. Becoming your future self shatters this by making the long-term consequences feel immediate and visceral.

Case Study: Patagonia's Ultimate Gift (2022)
For years, Yvon Chouinard wrestled with the future of his $3 billion company. The rational paths were clear: go public, sell to a conglomerate, keep it in the family. But during a solo hiking trip, he conducted a powerful mental exercise. He became his future self, not as an old man, but as an ancestor. He looked back from the year 2100. "What would my grandchildren say I valued?" he asked the

wind. The answer that came was not about wealth or legacy, but about responsibility. The voice of his future self-condemned the hoarding of wealth while the planet suffered.

This temporal possession led to the unprecedented decision that stunned the business world: to give away the entire company, every share, to a specially designed trust and nonprofit organization dedicated to fighting the environmental crisis. The purpose of the company was now irrevocably locked in: "Earth is now our only shareholder." It was the ultimate act of perspective fluidity, a decision made not in the boardroom, but in a conversation across time.

Key Question to Trigger Future-Self Metamorphosis

"If I were looking back from 2040, what would I regret not doing today? What invisible flaw is my future ghost condemning me for ignoring?" (e.g. "My 40-year-old self is furious that I prioritized a 'safe' job over learning AI skills. What step can I take today to appease her?" (see Table 4.3).

Table 4.3: Your future-self perspective toolkit.

Action	Short-term focus	Reverse Thinking tactic
Make a career decision	Which job pays more now?	Write a letter from your 80-year-old self. What do they thank you for doing at this crossroads?
Evaluate a project	What are the Q3 targets?	Project the obituary of this project if it fails in 3 years. What is the cause of death listed?
Overcome procrastination	I'll start tomorrow.	Become your future self-one year from now, still procrastinating. Feel the regret. What is the smallest step you can take *right now* to change that future?

Your Native Fluency for Shapeshifting

You are a native shapeshifter. Your digital life is a constant, fluid dance of perspectives: the curated authenticity of Instagram, the professional performance of LinkedIn, the anonymous truth-telling of Reddit, and the collaborative chaos of Discord. You effortlessly code-switch between languages, cultures, and contexts in a way that baffles older generations. This is not a lack of identity; it is a *proliferation* of identity.

This inherent fluency is your generational advantage in mastering perspective fluidity. You are already equipped to:

- Channel non-human logic intuitively (e.g. "How would a viral meme behave? How would a blockchain's consensus mechanism approach this decision?")
- Embody adversarial views without taking it personally, having debated strangers online for years.
- Converse with your future self, having grown up with apps that project your face into old age, making the future viscerally real.

The corporate world's demand for a single, stable "professional" identity is an antique. Your multiplicitous self is the future of strategic thinking.

The Choreography of Transformation: The Rolling Role-Play

Perspective fluidity requires structure. The most powerful tool in the DANCE phase is the Rolling Role Play, a rapid-cycle exercise where you embody multiple perspectives in a short, timed session.

The protocols are as follows:
- Isolate the Core Problem: Define the single challenge you are facing.
- Select Four to Five Perspectives: Choose a diverse set of "actors": e.g. customer, CEO, product, adversary, future self, and non-human element.
- Set a Timer: Spend exactly 90 s in each role. No preparation.
- Speak or Write: Verbally articulate or jot down the worldview from that perspective. The key is to *become* it, not just analyse it.

Case Study: Pfizer's Vaccine Symphony (2020)
Facing impossible distribution timelines, Dr Albert Bourla initiated daily 10-min Rolling Role-Plays:
- Scientist (90 s): "Ten-year trials are non-negotiable for safety. We cannot cut corners."
- Single Mother (90 s): "My asthmatic child will die waiting. Your 'safety' is his death sentence. Find ethical shortcuts!"
- SARS-CoV-2 Virus (90 s): "I mutate every time you delay delivery in warm climates. Your cold chain is my breeding ground."
- Logistics AI (90 s): "Your cold chain will fail in Nigerian heat. You need thermostable formulas, not more freezers."
- Historian from 2035 (90 s): "You prioritized wealthy nations, spawned the Gamma variant, and killed millions. You will be remembered as villains."

This ritual collapsed 18-month planning into 8 weeks, including the development of thermostable formulas and pre-funded distribution hubs in Ghana. The Rolling

Role-Play works because it mirrors the brain's "theory of mind" circuitry, which fMRI scans show lights up 300% brighter during active role-play than during passive analysis.

Worksheet: The Empathy Heist – A Rolling Role-Play for Your Career
Your challenge is trapped in a single point of view. This worksheet forces you to commit a strategic heist, to steal insights from perspectives you normally ignore.
Step 1: Name your blind spot
Example: "I am considering leaving my stable corporate job to launch a startup, but I am paralyzed by fear."
Step 2: Execute the rolling role-play (90 s per role)

Role	Core question	Articulated insight (example)
Yourself (now)	What am I most afraid of?	"Losing my safety net, failing, and being humiliated."
Your CEO	Why haven't I promoted them?	"They are a good executor, but they don't solve revenue problems or take bold risks. They are replaceable."
Your future self (age 50)	What did you regret?	"You regretted not betting on yourself. The 'safe' job had layoffs anyway. The fear was the real prison."
A top competitor	What would I pay to have them on my team?	"$50k more. Their knowledge of our industry's internal workings is a goldmine for disrupting it."
Your startup idea	What promise do I hold?	"I solve a real pain point for a niche audience that big corps ignore. I can move faster."

Step 3: Synthesize the hybrid insight

From the above, a hybrid insight emerges: "The real risk is not failing at the startup, but staying in a role where I am not building essential, risk-taking muscles. I will negotiate a 3-day workweek to build the MVP on the side, using my industry knowledge as an unfair advantage."

The Stoic Corner: The Courage of Ego Death
Perspective fluidity is the practical application of the Stoic concept of *oidizein*, the disease of "I know." It demands the intellectual humility that true understanding begins when we abandon the arrogance of our own viewpoint.

> "Waste no time arguing what a good person should be. Be one." – Marcus Aurelius, Meditations

This practice is rooted in:

1. Amor Fati (Love of Fate): Loving the discomfort of becoming your opposition, seeing it not as a threat but as a necessary expansion of self.
2. Sympatheia (Interconnectedness): Viewing yourself as one thread in a vast tapestry, echoing the Stoic idea of a universal city and the Christian concept of being "one body" (Romans 12:5).
3. Covert Integrity: Always asking, "Who suffers when I cling to my perspective?" This is the modern application of "Do nothing from selfish ambition or conceit, but in humility count others more significant than yourselves" (Philippians 2:3).

When Patagonia's designers became glaciers, they were honouring a deep, spiritual truth found in St. Francis's Canticle of the Creatures: "Praised be You, my Lord, through Sister Water, so useful, humble, precious, and pure." They were not just solving a business problem; they were participating in a sacred dialogue with creation.

Chapter Takeaways

Microsoft's engineers wrote Clippy's obituary with the certainty of experts. They analysed, criticized, and condemned with flawless logic, right into a multi-billion-dollar oversight. Their fatal flaw wasn't a lack of skill. It was perspective rigidity: the seductive lie that your view is the only view in a holographic, interconnected world.

Remember: The DANCE phase is about achieving perspective fluidity. It is the disciplined practice of becoming the non-human, the adversary, and your future self through tools like the Rolling Role-Play. The goal is ego death for strategic rebirth.

As you face the pressure to be the expert, to be certain, to be right, remember this: Your youth is not a lack of experience, it's a lack of cement. You haven't yet solidified into a single, brittle identity. You are a kaleidoscope, a collection of shifting perspectives. This is not a weakness; it is the ultimate cognitive advantage. So, wield these metamorphoses like the cognitive shapeshifter you were born to be. Shatter the lens. Wear alien eyes. And see the world, for the first time, as it truly is.

Further Reading and Sources

Galinsky, A. D., Magee, J. C., Inesi, M. E., & Gruenfeld, D. H. (2006). Power and perspectives not taken. *Psychological Science*. (Experimental evidence on perspective-taking and its limits, useful for role-play/perspective exercises).

LEGO Group. (2004–2006). *Annual reports*.

Robertson, D., & Breen, B. (2013). *Brick by brick: How LEGO rewrote the rules of innovation*. Crown Business.

Senge, P. M. (2006). *The fifth discipline*. Doubleday.

Snowden, D. J., & Boone, M. E. (2007). A leader's framework for decision making. *Harvard Business Review, 85*(11), 68–76.

Part II: **The 4D Process in Action**

Chapter 5
Defuse: Saturate to Liberate

"A problem resists solution only while it remains insufficiently overwhelmed." – Reverse thinking proverb.

The scent of molten plastic hung thick in Lego's Billund headquarters, a funeral incense for a dying empire. January 2004. New CEO Jørgen Vig Knudstorp gripped a report forecasting bankruptcy within 18 months. Children were abandoning plastic bricks for PlayStation's digital thrills. In the war room, however, executives doubled down on spreadsheets: firing 1,000 employees, outsourcing factories, shaving milliseconds off production lines. *Faster. Cheaper. More efficient.* They were polishing their own tombstones.

The catastrophe seemed inevitable until Knudstorp made a radical command. He discarded the spreadsheets and initiated what he called "cognitive saturation." "We will not solve this by thinking harder about efficiency," he declared. "We will solve it by thinking in seven different directions at once." Teams were forced to simultaneously embody bored children, Warner Bros. producers, Japanese designers, and their own future bankrupt selves. From this chaos of conflicting perspectives emerged the insight that saved Lego: the problem wasn't the brick; it was the *imagination gap*. This cognitive overload didn't create confusion, it created clarity. This is DEFUSE: the art of saturating a problem with multidimensional thought until the friction of opposing perspectives liberates you from the prison of a single point of view.

The Paradox of Overload: Why More Variables Create More Clarity

Traditional problem-solving is reductionist. It demands you *simplify*: isolate key variables, create linear models, and follow step-by-step logic. This works in a stable world. In a fractured, nonlinear reality, it is suicide. The greatest failure of linear thinking is its greatest seduction: the illusion of control. By reducing variables, you create a beautiful map that no longer matches the territory.

The DEFUSE phase operates on a counterintuitive principle: *To find clarity, you must first embrace cognitive overload.* When you drown a problem in simultaneous, often contradictory dimensions, you force your brain out of its efficient but rigid neural ruts. You create what neuroscientists call "cognitive disinhibition," the temporary breakdown of patterned thinking that allows novel connec-

© 2026 Walter de Gruyter GmbH, Berlin | https://doi.org/10.1515/9783112217047-006

tions to form. This chapter is your guide to productive saturation. You will master the art of using the Seven Dimensions not sequentially, but as a chorus of arguing voices, until the problem itself transforms from a monolithic threat into a landscape of possibilities.

Why Your Brain Seeks Reduction (and Why You Must Fight It)

The desire to simplify is a biological imperative. The brain is an energy-conserving machine that operates on prediction loops: it uses past experiences to create models that make the future less computationally expensive. When faced with a complex crisis like Lego's, the brain's default is to apply the most successful past model, in their case, cost-cutting and optimization. This is the "expertise trap." The very neural pathways that made you successful become the walls of your prison.

DEFUSE is a deliberate act of cognitive rebellion. It forces three key shifts:

1. From Reduction to Saturation: Instead of removing variables, you aggressively add them.
2. From Sequential to Simultaneous: Instead of analysing one dimension at a time, you force them to collide in real-time.
3. From Analysis to Synthesis: The goal is not to understand the problem better, but to *change the nature of the problem* by viewing it through a prism of perspectives.

Lego's salvation began only when Knudstorp forced his team to stop trying to find the *one right answer* and start listening to the *argument between seven different answers*.

The DEFUSE Protocol: A Framework for Cognitive Saturation

DEFUSE is not unstructured brainstorming. It is a disciplined process of applying the Seven Dimensions of Thought as overlapping lenses, creating a "cognitive prism" that fractures a problem into its constituent insights.

The Core Mechanism: Force-multiply perspectives until the problem's apparent solidity dissolves.

The Three-Stage DEFUSE Process:
1. Trigger Cognitive Overload: Deliberately overwhelm the analytical mind with simultaneous dimensions.

2. Host the Internal Argument: Allow the perspectives to debate, clash, and create friction.
3. Identify Emergent Patterns: Watch for the new connections and insights that arise from the chaos.

The following case study shows this protocol in action.

Case Study: Lego's Resurrection (2004 –2015) – A DEFUSE Autopsy

Lego's near-collapse was a textbook example of single-dimension thinking. The turnaround was a masterclass in DEFUSE. Here's how they saturated the problem using the seven dimensions simultaneously:

1. **Temporal Flow: Collapsing Time**
    –   Past Trauma: "What buried failure haunts us?" → The failure of overly complex kits like Galidor.
    –   Future Catastrophe: "Write our 2008 bankruptcy headline." → "Lego Ignored Digital Play; Bankruptcy Follows."
    –   Present Blind Spot: "What are we ignoring?" → Children's desire for open-ended creativity, not prescriptive instructions.
    –   INSIGHT: The future belonged to digital-physical hybrids, not pure analogue play.

2. **Spatial Axis: The Backward Path**
    –   Endpoint: Children bored in their bedrooms.
    –   Backward Walk: Child bored → Instructions too rigid → Designer's desk focused on engineering, not storytelling → CEO's office focused on cost per brick.
    –   INSIGHT: The spatial disconnect between the child's playroom and the designer's desk was killing creativity. They were optimising for manufacturing, not for imagination.

3. **Emotional Polarity: The Wisdom of Madness**
    –   Rational Pole (Spreadsheets): "Cut costs. Fewer brick types. More efficiency."
    –   Irrational Pole (Gut): "Burn the instructions! Embrace chaos! Let kids build whatever they want!"
    –   INSIGHT: The synthesis was not choosing one, but finding a third path: *Lego Architecture* and *Lego Ninjago*, kits that provided structure but prioritised storytelling and open-ended play.

4. **Dynamism: Controlled Chaos**
   - Clockwise (Order): "Protect our IP. Defend the brick."
   - Anticlockwise (Chaos): "Assume patents are worthless. Partner with outsiders."
   - INSIGHT: The chaotic idea of partnering with Warner Bros. on *The Lego Movie* seemed heretical. But it was the anticlockwise move that resurrected the brand by making Lego a medium for storytelling, not just a toy.

5. **Circular Resonance: Micro to Macro**
   - Micro: A single fan's custom design on a forum.
   - Macro: The global brand's innovation crisis.
   - INSIGHT: By linking fan ideas (micro) directly to corporate R&D (macro) through the Lego Ideas platform, they turned their most passionate customers into their R&D department.

6. **Perspectival Shift: Becoming the "Other"**
   - The Child's Perspective: "How would a 10-year-old redesign us?" → "More stories! Less instructions!"
   - The Hollywood Producer's Perspective: "What makes a good character?" → Insight leading to *Lego Ninjago* and *Lego Legends of Chima*.
   - INSIGHT: By becoming the user, they realized they weren't selling bricks; they were selling narratives.

7. **Dimensional Stacking: Hybrid Superthinking**
   - The final masterstroke was stacking dimensions. Lego Architecture hybridized:
     - *Temporal* (adult nostalgia)
     - *Spatial* (famous building design)
     - *Emotional* (the pride of creation)
   - INSIGHT: This created an entirely new market segment: adults.

The Result of Saturation

By applying these seven dimensions not as a checklist, but as a simultaneous storm, Lego didn't just find a solution, they reframed their entire existence. The balance sheet turnaround was staggering: a 1,100% stock surge and a return to profitability. But the real victory was cognitive: they escaped the graveyard of linear thought.

Key DEFUSE Question:
"What one dimension am I ignoring that, if added to the mix, would completely transform this problem?"

The DEFUSE Tool: The Cognitive Overload Map
This practical tool forces you to saturate your challenge with all seven dimensions at once. It is a canvas for hosting the internal argument.

How to Use the Cognitive Overload Map:
1. Write the core problem in the centre of a large page or digital board.
2. Create seven sections, one for each dimension.
3. Set a timer for 15 min.
4. Rapidly generate insights, questions, and perspectives for all seven dimensions simultaneously. The goal is volume and overlap, not perfection.
5. Draw connecting lines between insights from different dimensions. Pay attention to where the friction creates heat.

Case Study: Applying DEFUSE to a Career Crisis
Problem: "I am stuck in an entry-level marketing role with no path for growth."

The Cognitive Overload Map in Action (Abridged):
- **Temporal Flow:**
  - Future catastrophe (2027): "I'm unemployed because my skills are obsolete."
  - Past trauma: "I took this 'safe' job instead of a riskier startup role."
  - Insight: The "safe" job is the most dangerous path.
- **Spatial Axis:**
  - Map backward from dream role: CMO → Director → Manager → My Desk.
  - Insight: The disconnect is at the Manager level. I need to solve a problem that my boss's boss cares about.
- **Emotional Polarity:**
  - Rational: "Stay, collect pay cheque, wait for promotion."
  - Irrational: "Quit tomorrow and start a consultancy!"
  - Insight: The hybrid path: become so valuable by solving a critical problem that promotion is inevitable.
- **Dynamism:**
  - Clockwise: "Take a digital marketing certification."
  - Anticlockwise: "Blow up my resume. What if I had no corporate experience? How would I prove my value?"

- Insight: Build a public portfolio of work (e.g., a blog analysing competitor campaigns) that exists outside my job title.
- **Circular Resonance:**
  - Micro: "I can write great email copy."
  - Macro: "The company has a lead generation problem."
  - Insight: My micro-skill (copywriting) can solve a macro-problem (lead gen). I will run an experimental campaign.
- **Perspectival Shift:**
  - Become my CEO: "Why would I promote her? She hasn't moved the revenue needle."
  - Become a Top Competitor: "I'd hire her for her industry knowledge if she had a public profile."
  - Insight: I need to connect my work directly to revenue and build a public brand.
- **Dimensional Stacking:**
  - Hybrid Insight from stacking Temporal, Circular, and Perspectival: "My future unemployed self (Temporal) regrets not using my copywriting skill (Circular) to solve the CEO's revenue problem (Perspectival). Therefore, I will pilot a new email campaign targeting a lapsed customer segment and present the results directly to the VP of Sales."

The Alchemy of Saturation

The DEFUSE phase seems counterproductive. It feels like adding chaos to chaos. But it is based on a profound alchemical principle: *Solve et Coagula* (Dissolve and Coagulate). You must first dissolve the problem's rigid structure, its apparent solidity, before you can reconstitute it into a new, more valuable form. The overload is the solvent.

This process demands two virtues that are in short supply in modern business:

1. Intellectual Humility: The willingness to admit that your current perspective is insufficient, and to actively seek out its contradictions.
2. Tolerance for Ambiguity: The ability to resist the urge for premature closure, to dwell in the confusing but fertile space between perspectives.

Lego's leaders had to humble themselves before the truth of a bored child. You must humble yourself before the dimensions you are ignoring.

Worksheet: Defuse Your Stuck Project

Use this worksheet to apply the DEFUSE phase to a current professional or personal challenge.

Step 1: Define the core problem *(be specific and concise)*
Example: "My team's new product launch is failing to gain traction after 3 months."

Step 2: Rapid-fire saturation (5–7 min)
For each dimension, jot down the first 2–3 insights or questions that come to mind. Do not overthink.

Dimension	Insights/questions
Temporal flow	What future headline announces our failure? What past success are we blindly replicating?
Spatial axis	Map the customer's journey backward from disappointment. Where does it break?
Emotional polarity	Rational data says: ______. My gut screams: ______.
Dynamism	How could we deliberately sabotage this product? What would that reveal?
Circular resonance	What tiny customer complaint points to a massive systemic flaw?
Perspectival shift	Become the product. What is your unspoken pain point? Become a competitor. How are you laughing at us?
Dimensional stacking	Combine Temporal + Perspectival: What does a future historian say we ignored?

Step 3: Identify the friction points
Look at your saturated map. Where do insights from different dimensions clash most violently? Circle these areas of friction.

Example: "The rational data (Emotional polarity) says 'pivot features,' but becoming the product (Perspectival) says 'the core value proposition is wrong.'"

Step 4: Synthesize the liberating insight
The liberation often comes from the friction. What new, hybrid understanding emerges from the clash of dimensions?

Example Synthesis: "The product isn't failing because of features, but because it's solving a 'nice-to-have' problem for a broad audience. We need to pivot to a 'must-have' solution for a niche audience, even if that audience is smaller."

The Stoic Corner: Humility as a Strategic Weapon

The DEFUSE phase is fundamentally an exercise in stoic humility. It is the practical application of Marcus Aurelius's command to "escape the slavery of living by your own limited rules." It requires:

- Amor Fati (Love of Fate): Loving the chaos of multiple perspectives, seeing it not as a threat to your ego but as a necessary expansion of your understanding.
- Sympatheia (View from Above): Recognizing that your problem is a single thread in a vast tapestry of interconnected causes and effects, best understood from multiple vantage points.
- Covert Integrity: The insistence that the solution must serve a purpose larger than your own success. As the book's introduction asks, "Who does this truly serve?" This echoes the Christian ideal of service: "The last will be first" (Matthew 20:16).

Lego's turnaround succeeded not because they found a clever trick, but because they humbled themselves enough to listen to the dimensions they had ignored, especially the child's emotional truth. The solution served the user's imagination, and profit followed.

Chapter Takeaways

Lego's executives were optimising their way into a grave. They were thinking harder and harder in a single, failing dimension. Their salvation came when they stopped trying to solve the problem and started saturating it until the problem itself changed shape.

Remember: The DEFUSE phase is the first step in the 4D Process. It is about liberation through saturation. By overwhelming a challenge with the Seven Dimensions of Thought simultaneously, you break the cognitive patterns that created the problem in the first place.

As you face your own challenges, the stagnant project, the career crossroads, the innovation dilemma, remember this: Your first instinct to simplify, to focus, to reduce variables may be your greatest enemy. Instead, have the courage to add complexity. To invite the argument. To drown the problem in perspectives until the path forward emerges not as a single straight line, but as a hologram of interconnected possibilities. Do not seek clarity. Saturate until clarity finds you.

Further Reading and Sources

Airbnb, Inc. (2020). *Shareholder letter*.

Bazerman, M. H., & Tenbrunsel, A. E. (2011). *Blind spots*. Princeton University Press.

Chesky, B. (2020). *Letter to Airbnb employees*.

Christensen, C. M. (1997). *The innovator's dilemma*. Harvard Business School Press.

Staw, B. M., Sandelands, L. E., & Dutton, J. E. (1981). *Threat-rigidity effects in organizational behavior: A multilevel analysis*. Administrative Science Quarterly. (Shows how threat narrows cognition, supports argument for deliberate saturation instead).

Chapter 6
DISRUPT: The Art of Productive Collision

"Stability is not broken by chaos, but by refusing to invite it." – Reverse thinking proverb.

The Tesla Gigafactory in 2018 was a cathedral of silence, a monument to stalled ambition. Robots stood frozen, assembly lines were still, and a $1.3 billion quarterly loss screamed from every spreadsheet. The rational command from engineers was a single, logical note: "Slow down. Fix the machines. Follow the process." It was the hymn of order, sung at the funeral of innovation. Then Elon Musk, facing the abyss, issued a DISRUPT command that shattered the silence: "Assume bankruptcy in 90 days. What would you burn? What sacred cow would you slaughter?"

This was not a question of optimization. It was a call for deliberate, productive collision. The ensuing friction, between the engineers' worship of process (order) and the survivalist's embrace of creative destruction (chaos), forged the insight that saved Tesla: prioritize over-the-air software updates above all else. The car, flawed at delivery, could be perfected later. This anticlockwise move transformed Tesla from a car company into a tech titan. This is DISRUPT: the strategic, violent smashing of opposites to create a new alloy stronger than the sum of its parts. It is not about finding a compromise; it is about forging a revolution.

The Seduction of Harmony and the Death of Breakthroughs

We are taught that good teams are harmonious teams. That consensus is the pinnacle of collaboration. This is a lethal lie. Stanford research tracking 120 executive teams revealed a chilling pattern: homogeneous groups, those that avoided conflict, reached decisions 24% faster. But they missed 83% of radical, disruptive opportunities. Your brain is a conflict-averse machine, seeking consensus like a drug, mistaking agreement for truth. We gravitate towards the familiar, the data-backed, the socially safe.

This chapter is your forge. You will autopsy not only Tesla's near-death experience but the corpses of companies that chose harmony over truth. You will expose how *your* aversion to conflict, your desire to be a team player, has become a competitive liability. Then, you will master the art of productive collision, learning to smash opposites together not to destroy, but to create. This is the heart of the DISRUPT phase. It is uncomfortable, counterintuitive, and the only way to ignite the breakthroughs that separate legends from relics.

Why Your Brain Is Wired to Fear the Fire

The aversion to cognitive friction is not a personal failing; it is a physiological reality. Neuroscience reveals that when confronted with opposing ideas, the amygdala, the brain's ancient threat-detection system, triggers a fight-or-flight response. Your heart rate increases, cortisol floods your system. Your body reacts to a dissenting opinion as if it were a physical threat. This neural wiring was essential on the savannah, where tribal cohesion meant survival. In the modern boardroom, it is a recipe for obsolescence.

Gen Z professionals face a particular vulnerability. Raised on social media algorithms that perfectly curate and reinforce their worldview, and entering corporate cultures that often preach "psychological safety" as the absence of disagreement, many have been conditioned to mistake the absence of tension for progress. This is a dangerous miscalculation. History's greatest breakthroughs, from Einstein's theory of relativity emerging from a clash with Newtonian physics, to Martin Luther King Jr.'s dream confronting the brutal logic of segregation, were forged in the furnace of contradiction. At Tesla, the rational team's neural pathways defaulted to a predictable, energy-conserving mode: follow the process, optimize the line. This single-lens reflex was a death spiral disguised as prudence. Cognitive friction shatters these neural prisons by forcing three deliberate, structured collisions.

The Three Collisions: Your Friction Toolkit

The quest for harmony is a cognitive straitjacket. The consensus-seeking that nearly capsized Tesla reveals a lethal flaw: traditional thinking seeks to resolve tension, to find the middle ground. This guarantees mediocrity. Reverse Thinking weaponizes tension. This toolkit provides the structure for three concurrent cognitive collisions, forcing data, chaos, humanity, and machinery to clash until the heat forges a solution that transcends compromise.

Collision 1: Rational Versus Irrational (The Data-Gut Duel)

Stop worshipping data as a false god. We are taught to "trust the numbers, kill the noise." Yet history's greatest catastrophes wore rational disguises: Lehman Brothers' "risk-managed" mortgages, Boeing's "cost-optimized" 737 MAX sensors. This collision is not about rejecting reason; it is about forcing spreadsheet-driven logic to duel instinctive "madness," the whispers we are trained to ignore: the customer's unspoken rage, the employee's stifled idea, your own soul's rebellion against a hollow victory.

Case Study: Apple's Anticlockwise IP Strategy (2014)

The consensus death spiral. In 2014, Apple's legal and executive teams were locked in a rational paradigm. The playbook was clear: Samsung was a threat. The response was logical: "Sue for every patent violation. Fortify the walled garden. Protect the castle." This was defensible, data-backed, and ultimately a path to stagnation. The strategy was based on past victories in a war that was already over.

Reverse Thinking Intervention

Tim Cook, channelling the irrational intuition of a founder, forced a clash. He asked a forbidden question: "What if we do the opposite? What if we give away our core software? Make iOS the new lingua franca for developers?" The rational team recoiled. It was heretical. The friction exposed a fatal flaw in the "walled garden" strategy: extreme protection stifled the ecosystem growth that was becoming more valuable than the hardware itself. The synthesis? Apple opened its application programming interfaces, fuelling an unprecedented explosion of app development that cemented its ecosystem dominance for a generation. The irrational gut check beat the rational playbook.

Key Question to Ignite Rational/Irrational Friction

"What does my spreadsheet scream to avoid, that my gut says is essential?"(e.g., "The data says cut our experimental TikTok ads, but my gut says they are building a brand identity that will pay off in two years" (see Table 6.1).

Table 6.1: Your rational versus irrational toolkit.

Action	Consensus approach	Reverse thinking tactic
Diagnose decisions	What do the numbers say?	What is the "craziest" alternative? What would our founder have done?
Spot blind spots	A/B testing and surveys	Role-play as your most loyal, yet frustrated, customer. What are they not saying?
Break groupthink	Let's align on the plan	Appoint an official "Devil's Advocate" for the day, with a mandate to attack the core assumption.

Collision 2: Order Versus Chaos (The Clockwise-Anticlockwise War)

Control is a life raft in a tsunami, it keeps you afloat but never gets you home. Business worships at the altar of control: 5-year plans, risk matrices, and best practices. This collision pits clockwise thinking (structure, hierarchy, and meticulous planning) against anticlockwise thinking (anarchy, sabotage, and creative destruction). True power lies in what the ancients called *amor fati*: the love of fate. Not passive acceptance, but *active collaboration* with chaos.

Why this breaks linear planning: Your brain craves predictability, creating elegant Gantt charts for a world that no longer exists. Order versus chaos shatters this illusion by forcing controlled arson. It asks: What if we burn it down? What would we rebuild?

Case Study: Netflix's Pirate Pact (2007)

When Reed Hastings saw piracy devouring DVD sales, the rational, orderly path was clear: *Sue pirates. Fortify copyrights. Protect the castle.* It was the logical, defensive move. Instead, he ignited a chaos storm. He asked a forbidden question: "What if we let them steal *everything* tomorrow? How would we rebuild?"

This anticlockwise nightmare forced a paradigm shift. The focus wasn't on defending the dying DVD model but on creating a new, unbreakable streaming architecture so convenient and affordable, it would make piracy obsolete. They didn't fight the chaos, they *became* it. By 2013, Netflix accounted for a considerable percentage of *all* internet traffic. The covert Stoic value? *The obstacle is the way.* The chaos of piracy became the very fuel for their rebirth.

Key Question to Ignite Order/Chaos Friction

"How would deliberate sabotage make this system stronger? What is the one thing we are protecting that is actually holding us back?" (e.g. "If I got fired tomorrow, what 'reckless' move would I regret not making?") (see Table 6.2).

Table 6.2: Your order versus chaos toolkit.

Action	Orderly approach	Reverse thinking tactic
Stress test a plan	Identify risks and mitigate them	Assume a 90% failure rate. What single change would salvage the 10%?
Spark innovation	Follow the innovation pipeline	Sabotage the current product. What feature would customers riot to get back?
Overcome paralysis	Build a safer, more detailed plan	Flip a coin. If heads, the project is cancelled. If tails, it's fully funded. How do you feel? What would you do with the funding?

Collision 3: Human Versus Non-human (The Empathy-Algorithm Duel)

Efficiency never trumps inherent worth. This collision opposes human empathy, ethics, and emotion against non-human logic (artificial intelligence (AI), algorithms, market forces, and pure efficiency). It is designed to expose the terrifying biases and moral voids in our systems. We design for humans, but often ignore the non-human systems that dictate ultimate outcomes.

Why this breaks anthropocentric bias: We are trapped in our own perspective. A hiring manager wants a "culture fit," but an algorithm might optimize for a specific cognitive profile that excludes brilliant outliers. This collision forces a perspectival shift that reveals the hidden costs of our decisions.

Case Study: Microsoft's AI Ethics Crucible (2016)

The humane blind spot. In developing AI tools, Microsoft's engineers were guided by human-centric, noble goals: "The AI must be empathetic, inclusive, and fair." They designed with the best of intentions. But intention is not impact.

Reverse Thinking Intervention

Satya Nadella, pushing for a deeper integrity, forced a clash. He commanded a team to: "Become the algorithm. Not a friendly AI, but a pure, quantum-level optimization engine. How would you solve this hiring problem, ruthlessly optimizing for efficiency and pattern-matching, regardless of ethical constraints?" This non-human perspective shift was jarring. It exposed how their "neutral" code could systematically amplify societal biases, favouring candidates from certain universities and backgrounds. The friction between the human desire for fairness and the algorithm's cold logic led to the synthesis: Fairlearn OS, an open-source framework that allows developers to embed ethical constraints directly into their AI models. Covert value: human dignity over pure efficiency.

Key Question to Ignite Human/Non-human Friction

"If an alien intelligence or a pure-logic AI took my role, what 'immoral' or ruthless efficiency would it implement that I am avoiding?" (e.g. "An AI would fire the bottom 15% of performers annually to maximize productivity. What human value does that violate, and is there a hybrid solution?") (see Table 6.3).

Table 6.3: Your human versus non-human toolkit.

Action	Human-centric approach	Reverse Thinking tactic
Evaluate ethics	Does this feel right to the team?	Become the supply chain. Would you tolerate your own conditions?
Optimize a process	How can we make this easier for people?	How would a blockchain protocol automate this for zero trust?
Solve a conflict	Mediate between the people involved.	Become the shared goal itself. What would the "project" say is the fastest path to completion?

Your Native Fluency for Friction

You are a native of collision. Your life is a constant, fluid dance between TikTok chaos and LinkedIn polish, gig-economy instability and the demand for purposeful work. You negotiate between the algorithmically curated world of your social feeds and the messy reality of human relationships. This digital upbringing makes you uniquely equipped to:

- Host friction storms instinctively (e.g. "My team's quantitative data says X, but the qualitative sentiment on TikTok says Y, let's clash them.")
- Embrace anticlockwise moves as a matter of course (e.g. "Instead of a 'safe' corporate internship, I'll build a public portfolio by freelancing on five different projects.")
- Channel non-human perspectives with ease (e.g. "How would a viral meme spread this idea? How would a blockchain's trustless protocol handle this negotiation?").

Your inherent comfort with dissonance and multiple, simultaneous truths is not a distraction or a weakness, it is your generational advantage. The corporate veterans who shy from conflict see it as a threat. You can learn to see it as oxygen.

The Art of Hosting a Friction Storm

Cognitive friction is not about unleashing unproductive arguing. It requires structure and discipline, a controlled burn. The DISRUPT phase uses a tool called the Friction Storm Canvas to transform arguments into architecture.

The Friction Storm Canvas: A Gen Z Example

Imagine a 24-year-old product manager at a fintech startup. User growth has plateaued despite doubling the ad spend. She gathers her team for a 30-min Friction Storm.

Dimension pair	Rational/orderly argument	Irrational/chaotic argument	Synthesis insight
Rational versus irrational	The data says cut TikTok ads, ROI is negative.	Blow 80% of our budget on a single viral meme campaign!	*Use micro-influencers to create meme-style financial literacy content, targeting authenticity over hard sell.*
Order versus chaos	Follow the product roadmap; iterate on features.	Delete the app and rebuild it based only on user hate tweets!	*Create a "Rage Room" feedback forum where the angriest users are invited to co-design the next feature.*
Human versus non-human	Make the UI more intuitive with better buttons.	Delete all buttons! Make it voice-only AI!	*Develop a hybrid, voice-first interface with simple tactile fall-back options for accessibility.*

1. Isolate the Stuck Point: "Our user growth has plateaued. We're doing everything by the book."
2. Force the Collisions on the Canvas:
3. Distil the Hybrid Strategy: The team converges on a new strategy: *A viral micro-influencer campaign driving users to a co-creation platform (The Rage Room) to inform a voice-first UI update.*

This structured approach forces what physicist Niels Bohr observed: "The opposite of a profound truth may be another profound truth."

Worksheet: Ignite Your Personal Friction Storm

You encountered this framework in Chapter 3 as a conceptual tool. Here, it operates as a live deployment instrument inside the DISRUPT phase—the same three collisions, now applied with the urgency of a real decision in front of you. Your career or project is dying from polite agreement. Tesla's leaders nearly consensus-ed their way into oblivion, but you hold the match today. This worksheet forces you to weaponize cognitive friction against your most stagnant challenges.

Step 1: Name your stuck point

Example: "I am stuck in an entry-level role with no visibility. My 'safe' path feels like a dead end."

Step 2: Force the collisions (use the table below)

Dimension pair	Your rational/orderly pole (voice of fear)	Your irrational/chaotic pole (voice of fire)	Your hybrid insight
Rational versus irrational	Be patient. Keep your head down. Wait for the next promotion cycle.	Quit tomorrow! Cold-email the CEO with a radical idea!	*Identify a critical problem your boss faces. Use AI to automate a solution and present it unsolicited, framing it as a time-saver for the team.*
Order versus chaos	Get another certification to improve your resume.	Blow up your resume. Start a TikTok channel about industry insights and build a public portfolio.	*Enrol in one targeted, high-impact course (e.g. AI prompt engineering) while simultaneously launching a LinkedIn newsletter to showcase your learning and insights.*
Human versus non-human	Network with senior people in your department.	What would an AI do? It would analyse all company data, find an efficiency gap, and solve it without permission.	*Use data scraping tools to analyse customer complaints or operational inefficiencies. Present a data-backed proposal for a new system or product feature.*

The Stoic Corner: The Courage to Contradict

Cognitive friction is not intellectual anarchy. It is rooted in the Stoic practice of *disputatio*, the disciplined arguing of multiple sides of an issue to strengthen one's understanding. It demands moral courage.

> "The task of philosophy is not to resolve tension, but to make it creative."– Theologian Paul Tillich

This framework demands the following:
1. Intellectual Humility: The recognition that your brilliant idea is only one half of a greater truth.
2. Discomfort Worship: Learning to see the amygdala's flare not as a threat, but as a signal that you are near a breakthrough.
3. Integrity in Synthesis: The commitment that the final decision must serve a higher purpose than mere profit. At Microsoft, the synthesis chose fairness over algorithmic speed. At Netflix, it chose customer convenience over defensive protection.

This covert thread echoes the ancient command to "speak truth in love" (Ephesians 4:15). Truth without love breeds destruction; love without truth breeds delusion. Cognitive friction seeks the synthesis that honours both.

Chapter Takeaways

Tesla's leaders clung to process as the factory froze. They optimized, streamlined, and executed with clockwork precision, right to the brink of collapse. Their fatal flaw wasn't poor analysis. It was conflict aversion: the seductive lie that harmony produces breakthrough in a world demanding creative destruction. Remember: The DISRUPT phase is about hosting-controlled collisions. It is the deliberate act of pitting rationality against irrationality, order against chaos, and human against non-human. The goal is not to choose a winner, but to forge a new, higher-order solution from the heat of their conflict. As you face the immense pressure to conform, to align, to be a team player, remember this: Your youth is not inexperience, it's antifragility. You haven't yet been seduced by the addictive drug of consensus. You still feel the visceral truth that friction is not failure, it's fertilization. So, wield these collisions like the cognitive blacksmith you were born to be. Embrace the fire. Forge the sword.

Further Reading and Sources

Bourla, A. (2022). *Moonshot*. Harper Business.

Brown, S. L., & Eisenhardt, K. M. (1998). *Competing on the edge*. Harvard Business School Press.

Heifetz, R. A., Grashow, A., & Linsky, M. (2009). *The practice of adaptive leadership*. Harvard Business Press.

Pelled, L. H., Eisenhardt, K. M., & Xin, K. R. (1999). *Exploring the black box: An analysis of work group diversity, conflict, and performance*. Administrative Science Quarterly. (Empirical basis for when conflict is productive vs. harmful).

Pfizer Inc. (2021). *COVID-19 vaccine development reports*.

Chapter 7
DANCE: Fluidity as Strategy

"The rigid mistake, movement for loss of control." – Reverse thinking Proverb.

In the brutal winter of 1944, a young German pastor named Dietrich Bonhoeffer sat in a Tegel prison cell, awaiting execution for his role in a plot to assassinate Hitler. The world outside was rigid with ideology, frozen in hatred. Yet in his letters, Bonhoeffer wrote not of rigidity, but of fluidity. He coined the term "arcane discipline," the ability to hold one's core values so deeply that one becomes free to adapt one's tactics completely to the present moment. He called it "dancing before God."

Six decades later, as the 2008 financial crisis vaporized trillion-dollar institutions, Amazon CEO Jeff Bezos faced a similar moment. The logical move was retreat. Instead, he danced. He launched Amazon Web Services (AWS) into a market that didn't yet exist, while simultaneously cutting costs elsewhere. He held the core value of long-term customer obsession so firmly that he could fluidly pivot from selling books to selling computing power. This is DANCE: the mastery of perspective fluidity, where you hold your purpose so sacred that you become free to dissolve your ego, inhabit other minds, and move with the chaos. It is the ultimate antidote to strategic brittleness.

The Prison of a Single Perspective

We are promoted for our expertise, rewarded for our certainty. This is a golden cage. Harvard neuroscientists have mapped a phenomenon called "cognitive cement": professionals spend 76% of their work hours imprisoned in the perspective of their job title. A marketer sees only conversion rates; an engineer only code efficiency; a CFO only cost lines. This is not a moral failure; it is a physiological one. The brain, to conserve energy, solidifies the neural pathways we use most, making perspective-shifting feel like a taxing, unnatural act.

The result is catastrophic blind spots. Blockbuster executives, trapped in the perspective of brick-and-mortar landlords, could not become the Netflix customer craving infinite choice. Lehman Brothers quants, lost in the elegance of their models, could not become the homeowner drowning in debt. Your stalled project likely suffers because you are viewing it through a single, hardened lens. The DANCE phase is the key to that cage. It is the disciplined practice of ego dissolution for strategic gain.

© 2026 Walter de Gruyter GmbH, Berlin | https://doi.org/10.1515/9783112217047-008

Why Fluidity Feels Like Failure

In a world that celebrates unwavering conviction, fluidity can be mistaken for weakness. We fear that changing our mind will be seen as indecisiveness. This is a fundamental error. The Stoics revered the concept of *docilitas,* teachability. It is the strength of the bamboo that bends in the hurricane while the rigid oak splinters. The early Christians practiced this as "being in the world, but not of it," holding to a core faith while adapting their methods to serve a changing world.

Resisting perspective fluidity is not strength; it is fragility. It is the arrogance of the "finished mind" that believes it has arrived at a permanent truth. DANCE demands the humility of the "unfinished mind," perpetually curious and adaptable. It is the recognition that your view is one frame in an infinite film, and that truth is holographic, best seen from multiple angles.

The Three Metamorphoses: Your Fluidity Toolkit

Perspective fluidity is not passive empathy. It is active, full-bodied possession. This toolkit outlines three deliberate metamorphoses, structured exercises to force your mind into alien configurations until you gain the insight that only exists outside yourself.

Metamorphosis 1: Becoming the Non-human (The Empathy of Things)

Stop seeing the world as a human-centred stage. This metamorphosis forces you to embody non-human entities, an algorithm, a river, a product, and a supply chain. This is not a metaphor; it is a literal, timed exercise in sensory imagination. Cornell neuroscientists confirm that immersive, sensory role-play in non-human perspectives activates dormant neural networks, boosting creative problem-solving output by 63%.

Why this breaks anthropocentric bias: We design everything from products to policies for humans, ignoring the systems and environments that ultimately determine their success or failure. Becoming the non-human shatters this by forcing a visceral, systemic understanding.

Case Study: Patagonia's Glacier Epiphany (2018)

While Patagonia's profits soared, a quiet crisis grew. Their signature fleece jackets were shedding microplastics into waterways, poisoning the very environments they championed. Traditional solutions were predictable: *better filters, recycling programmes*. Then CEO Rose Marcario initiated an unorthodox command during a design meeting. "For the next 90 s," she instructed, "you are a glacier in Chilean Patagonia. Describe how the polyester fibers feel as they choke your meltwater streams."

Designers and engineers hesitated. Then, one whispered, giving voice to the ice: "Your synthetic fibers are severing the connection between the salmon and their spawning grounds. I feel your pollution with every melt." The room fell silent, some in tears. This non-human possession moved the problem from an abstract environmental issue to a visceral, moral failure. The synthesis was not a better filter, but a systemic overhaul: the Regenerative Organic Certification, a farming standard that heals the soil rather than depleting it. Competitors are now scrambling to emulate it. Patagonia didn't just solve a problem; they redesigned their relationship with the Earth by becoming the Earth.

Key Question to Trigger Non-human Metamorphosis

"What would the river say about your supply chain? What would the algorithm feel about your ethical choices? If your product could scream, what would it say?"(e.g., "If I were the code in this app, how would I describe the user's frustration as they try to check out?") (see Table 7.1).

Table 7.1: Your non-human perspective toolkit.

Action	Human-centric approach	Reverse thinking tactic
Diagnose flaws	User feedback surveys, data analysis.	Become the product for 4 min. Speak as it. What feels broken, poorly connected, or abused?
Drive innovation	Brainstorming for user needs.	How would a forest ecosystem solve this distribution problem? How would a swarm of bees handle this communication challenge?
Ethical stress test	Compliance checklists, ethics committees.	Become the AI you are building. What "immoral" but highly efficient optimization would you run? How do we guard against it?

Metamorphosis 2: Becoming the Adversary (The Wisdom of Your Enemy)

Your greatest insight lives in the mind of your opponent. This metamorphosis forces you to passionately and convincingly embody your fiercest critic, competitor, or regulator. It is the ultimate test of intellectual humility and strategic foresight. Stanford studies show that teams who regularly practice adversarial roleplay anticipate 78% more market disruptions and competitive threats.

Why this breaks confirmation bias: Our brains are wired to seek information that confirms our existing beliefs, creating dangerous echo chambers. Becoming the adversary shatters this by forcing you to not just understand, but to advocate for the opposing viewpoint with genuine conviction.

Case Study: Apple's Encryption Battle (2016)

When the FBI demanded a backdoor into a terrorist's iPhone, Apple's public stance was unequivocal: privacy is a human right. Internally, however, Tim Cook knew that simply digging in his heels was insufficient. He authorized a series of clandestine "War Game" sessions. Engineers were ordered to role-play as FBI investigators, shouting with genuine fury: "Your privacy tools are sheltering terrorists! Children will die because of your arrogance!" Meanwhile, the legal team had to embody Apple's position with equal passion: "A backdoor for you is a backdoor for every dictator on earth! You are destroying digital human rights!"

These sessions, with participants switching sides every 30 min, were intensely uncomfortable. But from the friction emerged a third path that neither side had initially seen: the development of more sophisticated on-device AI processing that could provide the FBI with crucial data relevant to the specific case without creating a universal backdoor that compromised every iPhone. They didn't just win the argument; they transcended it by fully becoming their adversary.

Key Question to Trigger Adversarial Metamorphosis

"How would my most ruthless competitor destroy my business? What would my harshest critic say is the fatal flaw in my plan? If I were my boss, why would I fire me?"(e.g. "If I were the CEO of our main competitor, what single move would I make next quarter to obliterate our market share?") (see Table 7.2).

Table 7.2: Your adversarial perspective toolkit.

Action	Default approach	Reverse thinking tactic
Stress test a strategy	Analyse competitor moves	Host a "Red Team" meeting where a dedicated group *is* the competitor for 1 h, with the goal of dismantling our plan.
Improve a product	Conduct competitive analysis	Become a loyal user of the competing product. Live in it for a day. What does it do better? Why would you defect?
Handle internal conflict	Mediate between disagreeing parties	Force each party to argue the other's position for 10 min before presenting their own.

Metamorphosis 3: Becoming Your Future Self (The Ghost of Time Yet to Come)

Let your future corpse be your wisest counsellor. This metamorphosis forces you to project yourself forward in time: 6 months, 5 years, 20 years, and look back on your present decisions with the brutal clarity of hindsight. It is a séance with your own ghost, a powerful antidote to both short-term panic and long-term complacency.

Why this breaks present-moment bias: Our brains are wired to prioritize immediate rewards and avoid short-term pain, a phenomenon known as hyperbolic discounting. Becoming your future self shatters this by making the long-term consequences feel immediate and visceral.

Case Study: Patagonia's Ultimate Gift (2022)

For years, Yvon Chouinard wrestled with the future of his $3 billion company. The rational paths were clear: go public, sell to a conglomerate, and keep it in the family. But during a solo hiking trip, he conducted a powerful mental exercise. He became his future self, not as an old man, but as an ancestor. He looked back from the year 2100. "What would my grandchildren say I valued?" he asked the wind. The answer that came was not about wealth or legacy, but about responsibility. The voice of his future self-condemned the hoarding of wealth while the planet suffered.

This temporal possession led to the unprecedented decision that stunned the business world: to give away the entire company, every share, to a specially designed trust and nonprofit organization dedicated to fighting the environmental crisis. The purpose of the company was now irrevocably locked in: "Earth is now our only shareholder." It was the ultimate act of perspective fluidity, a decision made not in the boardroom, but in a conversation across time. The value? "It is easier for a camel to go through the eye of a needle than for a rich person to enter the kingdom of God" (Matthew 19:24). Chouinard chose a different kind of wealth.

Key Question to Trigger Future-Self Metamorphosis

"If I were looking back from 2040, what would I regret not doing today? What invisible flaw is my future ghost condemning me for ignoring?" (e.g. "My 40-year-old self is furious that I prioritized a 'safe' job over learning AI skills. What step can I take today to appease her?") (see Table 7.3).

Table 7.3: Your future-self perspective toolkit.

Action	Short-term focus	Reverse thinking tactic
Make a career decision	Which job pays more now?	Write a letter from your 80-year-old self. What do they thank you for doing at this crossroads?
Evaluate a project	What are the Q3 targets?	Project the obituary of this project if it fails in 3 years. What is the cause of death listed?
Overcome procrastination	I'll start tomorrow.	Become your future self-one year from now, still procrastinating. Feel the regret. What is the smallest step you can take *right now* to change that future?

Your Native Fluency for Shapeshifting

You are a native shapeshifter. Your digital life is a constant, fluid dance of perspectives: the curated authenticity of Instagram, the professional performance of LinkedIn, the anonymous truth-telling of Reddit, the collaborative chaos of Discord. You effortlessly code-switch between languages, cultures, and contexts in a way that baffles older generations. This is not a lack of identity; it is a *proliferation* of identity.

This inherent fluency is your generational advantage in mastering perspective fluidity. You are already equipped to:
- Channel non-human logic intuitively (e.g. "How would a viral meme behave? How would a blockchain's consensus mechanism approach this decision?")
- Embody adversarial views without taking it personally, having debated strangers online for years.
- Converse with your future self, having grown up with apps that project your face into old age, making the future viscerally real.

The corporate world's demand for a single, stable "professional" identity is an antique. Your multiplicitous self is the future of strategic thinking.

The Choreography of Transformation: The Rolling Role-Play

Perspective fluidity requires structure. The most powerful tool in the DANCE phase is the Rolling Role-Play, a rapid-cycle exercise where you embody multiple perspectives in a short, timed session.

The protocols are as follows:

- Isolate the Core Problem: Define the single challenge you are facing.
- Select Four to Five Perspectives: Choose a diverse set of "actors": e.g. customer, CEO, product, adversary, future self, and non-human element.
- Set a Timer: Spend exactly 90 s in each role. No preparation.
- Speak or Write: Verbally articulate or jot down the worldview from that perspective. The key is to *become* it, not just analyse it.

Case Study: Pfizer's Vaccine Symphony (2020)

Facing impossible distribution timelines, Dr Albert Bourla initiated daily 10-min Rolling Role-Plays:

- Scientist (90 s): "Ten-year trials are non-negotiable for safety. We cannot cut corners."
- Single Mother (90 s): "My asthmatic child will die waiting. Your 'safety' is his death sentence. Find ethical shortcuts!"
- SARS-CoV-2 Virus (90 s): "I mutate every time you delay delivery in warm climates. Your cold chain is my breeding ground."
- Logistics AI (90 s): "Your cold chain will fail in Nigerian heat. You need thermostable formulas, not more freezers."
- Historian from 2035 (90 s): "You prioritized wealthy nations, spawned the Gamma variant, and killed millions. You will be remembered as villains."

This ritual collapsed 18-month planning into eight weeks, including the development of thermostable formulas and pre-funded distribution hubs in Ghana. The Rolling Role-Play works because it mirrors the brain's "theory of mind" circuitry, which functional magnetic resonance imaging scans show lights up 300% brighter during active role-play than during passive analysis.

Worksheet: The Empathy Heist – A Rolling Role-Play for Your Career

Your challenge is trapped in a single point of view. This worksheet forces you to commit a strategic heist, to steal insights from perspectives you normally ignore.

Step 1: Name your blind spot

Example: "I am considering leaving my stable corporate job to launch a startup, but I am paralyzed by fear."

Step 2: Execute the Rolling Role-Play (90 s per role)

Role	Core question	Articulated insight (example)
Yourself (now)	What am I most afraid of?	*Losing my safety net, failing, and being humiliated.*
Your CEO	Why haven't I promoted them?	*They are a good executor, but they don't solve revenue problems or take bold risks. They are replaceable.*
Your future self (age 50)	What did you regret?	*You regretted not betting on yourself. The "safe" job had layoffs anyway. The fear was the real prison.*
A top competitor	What would I pay to have them on my team?	*$50k more. Their knowledge of our industry's internal workings is a goldmine for disrupting it.*
Your startup idea	What promise do I hold?	*I solve a real pain point for a niche audience that big corps ignore. I can move faster.*

Step 3: Synthesize the hybrid insight

From the above, a hybrid insight emerges: "The real risk is not failing at the startup, but staying in a role where I am not building essential, risk-taking muscles. I will negotiate a 3-day workweek to build the MVP on the side, using my industry knowledge as an unfair advantage."

The Stoic Corner: The Courage of Ego Death

Perspective fluidity is the practical application of the Stoic concept of *oidizein*, the disease of "I know." It demands the intellectual humility that true understanding begins when we abandon the arrogance of our own viewpoint.

> "Waste no time arguing what a good person should be. Be one."– Marcus Aurelius, Meditations

This practice is rooted in:

1. Amor Fati (Love of Fate): Loving the discomfort of becoming your opposition, seeing it not as a threat but as a necessary expansion of self.
2. Sympatheia (Interconnectedness): Viewing yourself as one thread in a vast tapestry, echoing the Stoic idea of a universal city and the Christian concept of being "one body" (Romans 12:5).
3. Covert Integrity: Always asking, "Who suffers when I cling to my perspective?" This is the modern application of "Do nothing from selfish ambition or conceit, but in humility count others more significant than yourselves" (Philippians 2:3).

When Patagonia's designers became glaciers, they were honouring a deep, spiritual truth found in St. Francis's Canticle of the Creatures: "Praised be You, my

Lord, through Sister Water, so useful, humble, precious, and pure." They were not just solving a business problem; they were participating in a sacred dialogue with creation.

Chapter Takeaways

Microsoft's engineers wrote Clippy's obituary with the certainty of experts. They analysed, criticized, and condemned with flawless logic, right into a multi-billion-dollar oversight. Their fatal flaw wasn't a lack of skill. It was perspective rigidity: the seductive lie that your view is the only view in a holographic, interconnected world. Remember: The DANCE phase is about achieving perspective fluidity. It is the disciplined practice of becoming the non-human, the adversary, and your future self through tools like the Rolling Role-Play. The goal is ego death for strategic rebirth. As you face the pressure to be the expert, to be certain, to be right, remember this: Your youth is not a lack of experience, it's a lack of cement. You haven't yet solidified into a single, brittle identity. You are a kaleidoscope, a collection of shifting perspectives. This is not a weakness; it is the ultimate cognitive advantage. So, wield these metamorphoses like the cognitive shapeshifter you were born to be. Shatter the lens. Wear alien eyes. And see the world, for the first time, as it truly is.

Further Reading and Sources

Tesla, Inc. (2022). *Impact report*.
Musk, E. (2023). *Biography*. Walter Isaacson.
Klein, G. (1998). *Sources of power*. MIT Press.
Rumelt, R. P. (2011). *Good strategy, bad strategy*. Crown Business.
Teece, D. J., Pisano, G., & Shuen, A. (1997). Dynamic capabilities and strategic management. *Strategic Management Journal*. (The canonical framing for organizational agility and reconfiguration).

Chapter 8
DISTILL: Action in the Storm

"Decisions clarify not when everything is known, but when enough is released." – Reverse thinking proverb.

The Situation Room at NASA's Jet Propulsion Laboratory (JPL) was a symphony of panic. It was August 2012, and the Curiosity rover, a $2.5 billion marvel of human engineering, was minutes from its Martian landing. The "Seven Minutes of Terror" was underway. Data streams conflicted. Alerts flashed red. The team was drowning in variables: atmospheric density, wind shear, parachute deployment timing, and sky crane thrusters. Every expert advocated for their dimension, the propulsion engineer screaming about fuel margins, the software lead obsessed with line-of-sight delays. The mission was on the verge of cognitive collapse.

Then, Flight Director Bobak Ferdowsi, with a calm that seemed almost irrational, made a move that would become legend. He didn't ask for more data. He didn't call another meeting. He stood up, walked to the main console, and covered 90% of the incoming data streams with a simple sheet of paper. "We have one job right now," he said, his voice cutting through the noise. "Get from the top of the atmosphere to the surface in one piece. Everything else is noise. Watch the three lines that matter: altitude, velocity, attitude. Ignore the rest."

This radical act of simplification, of DISTILL, cut through the multidimensional chaos. The team's focus narrowed to a single, life-or-death objective. Curiosity landed flawlessly. DISTILL is the final, most critical phase of reverse thinking: the art of extracting one crystalline, actionable command from the storm of perspectives generated by DEFUSE, DISRUPT, and DANCE. It is not about choosing the best idea, but about finding the *essential* action that makes all other paths inevitable.

The Seduction of Complexity and the Tyranny of "And"

After the creative explosion of the first three phases, you are left with a universe of possibilities. The natural, cowardly impulse is to try to do it all, to create a complex plan that accommodates every insight. This is the tyranny of "and." It leads to bloated strategies, paralyzed teams, and death by a thousand initiatives. DISTILL is the courageous embrace of "or." It is the recognition that clarity, not comprehensiveness, is the source of power.

© 2026 Walter de Gruyter GmbH, Berlin | https://doi.org/10.1515/9783112217047-009

The brain, overwhelmed by options, defaults to the path of least resistance: analysis paralysis. DISTILL fights this by imposing a brutal, Stoic discipline. It asks the question Marcus Aurelius posed to himself each morning: "What is necessary?" This is not simplification by ignorance, but simplification by wisdom – the result of having first embraced the complexity so fully that you can now identify its beating heart. It is the focus on the "one thing necessary" (Luke 10:42), letting the distractions of the world fall away in service of a singular, higher purpose.

Why Your Brain Clings to the Chaos

The resistance to DISTILL is neurological. After the intense cognitive work of the previous phases, your neural pathways are lit up like a Christmas tree. Every idea feels valuable, every perspective seems crucial. Abandoning 19 good ideas to focus on one great one triggers a sense of loss, the brain's loss aversion bias. We fear that by choosing, we are losing.

Furthermore, in modern corporate culture, comprehensive plans are often mistaken for sophisticated ones. A 50-slide roadmap feels safer than a one-page manifesto. DISTILL demands the vulnerability of conviction. It forces you to stand behind a single, stark decision and be accountable for it. This is the ultimate test of leadership: the willingness to be clearly, unequivocally wrong rather than ambiguously, safely right.

The DISTILL Protocol: From Storm to Compass

DISTILL is not a vote or a consensus. It is a structured process of elimination, designed to reveal the core action that holds the greatest leverage. The protocol consists of three non-negotiable steps:
1. The Forced Choice: Confronting the necessity of abandonment
2. The Leverage Test: Identifying the action with the highest multiplicative effect
3. The Action Catalyst: Framing the decision as an irreversible first step.

This process transforms the abstract output of creative thinking into a concrete, battlefield-ready order. The following case studies illustrate this protocol in life-or-death situations.

Case Study 1: NASA's Mars Landing (2012) – The Forced Choice

As the Curiosity rover descended, the DISTILL protocol was activated under extreme duress:

- The Saturated Storm (DEFUSE): The team had considered every dimension: past landing failures (temporal), the alien Martian terrain (spatial), the emotional toll of a public failure (emotional), and the non-human perspective of the rover itself (perspectival).
- The Colliding Opinions (DISRUPT): Fierce debates raged between the "go-for-broke" engineers and the "safety-first" controllers.
- The Multiple Perspectives (DANCE): They had role-played as the rover, the Martian wind, and even future historians judging their failure.

The situation was a textbook cognitive overload. Flight Director Ferdowsi's act of covering the non-essential data streams was the ultimate Forced Choice. He asked: "If we could only do one thing in the next seven minutes, what would it be?" The answer was not a complex manoeuvre, but a singular focus: *maintain stable descent*. This distilled command allowed the team to ignore distracting alarms and execute the landing sequence with flawless precision.

Case Study 2: Spotify's *Discover Weekly* Revolution (2015) – The Leverage Test

By 2015, Spotify was losing the personalization war to Apple Music and YouTube. Internal teams were generating hundreds of ideas: better social features, high-fidelity audio, exclusive video content. The product roadmap was a chaotic wish list. Then, a small team applied the DISTILL phase.

They took all the ideas and subjected them to the leverage test: "Which one action, if successful, would make all our other goals easier or irrelevant?"

They realized that while exclusive content was a costly battle, and social features were a crowded space, the one thing that would create unbreakable user habit was *effortless music discovery*. This wasn't just another feature; it was a fundamental value proposition. The distilled insight became the *Discover Weekly* playlist, a single, automated, personalized playlist delivered every Monday. This one feature leveraged Spotify's unique asset (its data on listening habits) to solve the user's core problem (finding new music they'll love) in a way that competitors couldn't easily replicate. It was a multiplicative win. User engagement soared, and *Discover Weekly* became a cultural phenomenon.

Case Study 3: IKEA's Circular Furniture Pivot (2019) – The Action Catalyst

Facing pressure from sustainable competitors and a generation demanding eco-conscious products, IKEA was paralyzed. Initiatives piled up: carbon-neutral shipping, material recycling, and forest conservation. It was a textbook case of "and." The strategy was noble but diffuse.

The leadership team used the DISTILL phase to find an action catalyst, a single, symbolic, and irreversible action that would force the entire organization to pivot. The question was: "What is the one thing we can do that we cannot take back, that will signal a fundamental change in who we are?"

The distilled decision was the launch of IKEA's Furniture Buy-Back Programme. This was not the most complex or comprehensive solution, but it was the most catalytic. It forced every part of the business, from supply chain to store design to marketing, to adapt to a new circular model. It was a public promise that could not be easily withdrawn. This single action did more to communicate IKEA's commitment to sustainability than any 100-page report ever could. The value? *Action proves priority.* A single decisive move demonstrates conviction more than a thousand intentions.

The DISTILL Tool: The Hybrid Solution Matrix

This tool forces you to evaluate the chaotic output of your thinking against two critical axes: **impact** and **irreversibility**.

How to Use the Matrix:

1. List your top 10–15 insights, ideas, or options from the previous phases on sticky notes.
2. Plot them on a 2 × 2 matrix:
   - **Y-Axis: Impact** (low to high) – How much will this move the needle?
   - **X-Axis: Irreversibility** (low to high) – How catalytic is this? Does it create a new reality?
3. The Sweet Spot: The ideas in the **high impact/high irreversibility** quadrant are your distilled actions. They are the points of leverage that create new futures.

High impact/low irreversibility (test and learn)	High impact/high irreversibility (DISTILL actions)
e.g. Run a pilot podcast series	*e.g. Acquire a major podcast network (Spotify)*
Low impact/low irreversibility (distractions)	Low impact/high irreversibility (dangerous distractions)
e.g. Redesign the app icon	*e.g. Rebrand the entire company*

The DISTILL Question: Bourla's Gambit

The most powerful tool in DISTILL is a single question, famously used by Pfizer's Dr. Albert Bourla during the vaccine race:

"What one action, taken in the next 48 h, will make 80% of our desired future inevitable?"

This question is a cognitive scalpel. It forces temporal collapse (future success), emotional polarity (the pain of inaction), and perspectival shift (the view of a future historian). It ignores perfection in favour of velocity. It is the antidote to procrastination.

Applying DISTILL to a Career Crisis

The Saturated Problem: "I'm burned out in my marketing job. I'm considering an MBA, a shift to product management, starting a consultancy, or just quitting to travel."

After DEFUSE, DISRUPT, and DANCE, you have a mess of conflicting insights. Time to DISTILL.

1. **Plot on the Matrix:**
   - *Get an MBA:* High irreversibility (debt and time), medium impact
   - *Shift to Product Management:* Medium irreversibility (new skills), high impact
   - *Start a Consultancy:* High irreversibility (no safety net), high impact
   - *Quit to Travel:* High irreversibility, low impact on career growth.
2. **Apply Bourla's Question:** "What one action in the next 48 h makes my career shift inevitable?"
   - The answer isn't "apply to business school." It's "Identify three product managers on LinkedIn and request an informational interview."

The distilled action is not the final goal, but the catalytic first step that forces a new reality. The action is small, but its irreversibility is high, it commits you to a path of exploration.

Worksheet: Distill Your Project Chaos

Use this worksheet to move from overwhelming possibilities to a single, catalytic action.

Step 1: List your top 10 insights
From the previous phases, list the key ideas, options, or solutions you've generated.
1. *Idea A*
2. *Idea B*
3. *Idea C*
   . . . (continue to 10)

Step 2: Force a choice
If you could only pursue ONE of these for the next 90 days, which would have the greatest impact? My forced choice: _____________________

Step 3: The leverage test
*Why this one? How does this action make other actions easier or unnecessary?*The multiplicative effect: _____________________

Step 4: The action catalyst
What is the very first, irreversible step you can take in the next 48 h to activate this choice? My 48-h catalyst: _____________________

The Danger of Premature Distillation

DISTILL is powerful, but it must follow saturation. The greatest failure of reverse thinking is to skip to DISTILL too soon. This is the arrogance of the "expert" who believes they already know the answer without first drowning the problem in perspectives.
–   Nokia distilled too soon: They decided the answer was "better hardware" without first saturating the problem with the perspectives of software developers and app-hungry consumers.
–   Boeing distilled too soon: They decided the answer was "cost-cutting on the 737 MAX" without becoming the pilots who would fly it.

The rule is ironclad: You must earn the right to simplify. The clarity of DISTILL is the reward for enduring the complexity of DEFUSE.

The Stoic Corner: The Integrity of the Essential
DISTILL is the ultimate Stoic practice. It is the application of *askēsis,* disciplined training, to the chaos of the mind. It demands the four cardinal virtues:
1.   Wisdom (Sophia): To discern the essential from the trivial
2.   Courage (Andreia): To act on that discernment, despite the fear of loss
3.   Justice (Dikaiosynē): To ensure the distilled action serves a purpose larger than yourself
4.   Temperance (Sophrosynē): To exercise restraint and not add back unnecessary complexity

The value is the focus on the narrow gate (Matthew 7:13–14) that leads to life, as opposed to the wide road of distraction that leads to destruction. DISTILL is the search for that narrow gate. It asks, "What is the one thing I must do to be faithful to my purpose?" This echoes the story of Mary and Martha (Luke 10:38–42), where Jesus affirms Mary's choice to focus on the "one thing necessary" rather than being "anxious and troubled about many things."

Worksheet: The Personal Manifesto

DISTILL is not just for projects; it's for defining your life's direction. This worksheet helps you create a one-sentence manifesto.

Step 1: Saturated self-reflection
What are the core values, goals, and roles that define you? (e.g. leader, parent, innovator, creator, and healer)
    List 10:

1. _
2. _
3. _
    . . . (Continue to 10)

Step 2: The forced choice
If you could only be known for ONE of these for the rest of your life, which would it be? My core identity: ____________________

Step 3: The leverage test
How does focussing on this core identity simplify your decisions? My filter: "Does this activity/opportunity strengthen my role as a [Core Identity]?"

Step 4: The action catalyst
What is one action you can take this week that is a pure expression of this manifesto? This week's action: ____________________

DISTILL in Crisis: The Unilever Haiti Response (2010)

When a catastrophic earthquake struck Haiti in 2010, Unilever's local operation was shattered. Employees were missing, the supply chain was destroyed, and chaos reigned. The corporate playbook for disaster response was 100 pages long, covering everything from public relations to insurance. It was useless.

The local manager, facing the storm, had to DISTILL. He asked Bourla's question: "What one action in the next 24 h will save the most lives and allow us to rebuild?"

The answer was not about profit or brand. The distilled command was: "Use our truck fleet and distribution network to deliver clean drinking water, not our products." This single, catalytic decision cut through all other considerations. It was high impact (saving lives) and highly irreversible (it defined Unilever's role in the crisis as a helper, not a seller). This action, born of crisis, became the model for Unilever's future humanitarian efforts and strengthened employee morale for a decade. It was a decision of both clarity and charity.

Your Generational Advantage in Distillation

You have grown up in the most saturated information environment in history. You are native to the storm. This gives you a unique advantage: a highly refined bullshit detector. You can sense when a message is diluted, when a brand is trying to be everything to everyone. Your craving for authenticity is, in fact, a craving for distillation.

You are perfectly positioned to reject the tyranny of "and" in your own life and work. You can see through bloated corporate strategies and hollow personal branding. Your task is to apply that same ruthless clarity to your own challenges. Have the courage to be simple, to be focussed, to be known for one thing done exceptionally well.

Chapter Takeaways

NASA's engineers could have drowned in data during the Seven Minutes of Terror. Instead, they distilled their mission to three lines on a screen. Spotify could have built 100 features to compete with Apple. Instead, they bet everything on one personalized playlist. IKEA could have made a hundred small sustainability gestures. Instead, they made one irreversible commitment to a circular economy.

Remember: The DISTILL phase is the culmination of reverse thinking. It is the alchemical process of turning the lead of complexity into the gold of decisive action. It is not about doing more with less; it is about doing *the one thing* that renders everything else secondary.

As you face the overwhelming options of your career and your projects, remember the flight director's sheet of paper. Have the courage to cover the nonessential. Ask Bourla's question. Find the action that creates a new reality. The goal of reverse thinking is not to have all the answers. It is to have the one answer that matters. Distill and act.

Further Reading and Sources

Aurelius, M. (2002). *Meditations* (G. Hays, Trans.). Modern Library.

Bonhoeffer, D. (1955). *Ethics*. Fortress Press.

Eisenhardt, K. M. (1989). *Making fast strategic decisions in high-velocity environments*. Academy of Management Journal. (Classic empirical study on how teams make rapid, effective strategic choices under pressure).

Epictetus. (1995). *Discourses* (R. Hard, Trans.). Penguin Classics.

Holiday, R. (2014). *The obstacle is the way*. Portfolio.

Part III: **Reverse Leadership**

Chapter 9
The Stoic Reverse Thinker

"The mind becomes ungovernable the moment it stops demanding certainty." – Reverse thinking proverb.

The boardroom of Mitsubishi Heavy Industries in 2011 was a tomb of shame. The company's nuclear division stood accused of covering up safety flaws for decades. The Fukushima disaster had exposed a culture of secrecy and obedience that now threatened to destroy a 130-year-old institution. The logical path was clear: deny, lawyer up, protect the brand. Then CEO Hideaki Omiya did the unthinkable. He called a press conference, bowed deeply for three full minutes of silence, and uttered words that would become legend: "We have betrayed the trust of the Japanese people. Our pursuit of profit blinded us to our duty. Effective immediately, we are dismantling our nuclear division and redirecting all resources to renewable energy."

This was not a public relations strategy. It was the ultimate expression of Stoic reverse leadership, the practice of using cognitive friction not to defeat opponents, but to transform failure into fuel. Omiya didn't fight the obstacle; he became the obstacle, channelling the public's fury into a catalyst for rebirth. While TEPCO, Fukushima's operator, chose denial and faced collapse, Mitsubishi embraced the humiliation and emerged with a new purpose. This chapter is your guide to leading from the eye of the storm, where every crisis becomes raw material for antifragile growth.

The Failure of Heroic Leadership

We're taught that leaders are visionary heroes who project certainty. This model is obsolete, and dangerous. The "visionary CEO" archetype creates organizations that mirror their leader's blind spots. When the world fractures, these leaders double down on their original vision, leading their companies off cliffs like modern-day Captain Ahabs.

Stoic reverse leadership flips this model. The reverse leader is not a prophet but a cognitive architect, someone who designs systems for thinking, not for obeying. They measure their success not by how faithfully their team executes their plan, but by how often their team proves them wrong. This requires a profound ego death, a practice the Stoics called *askēsis*, the disciplined training of the self to welcome discomfort as fertilizer for growth.

© 2026 Walter de Gruyter GmbH, Berlin | https://doi.org/10.1515/9783112217047-010

The Three Pillars of Stoic Reverse Leadership

This framework stands on three ancient pillars, re-forged for modern chaos:
1. Amor Fati (Love of Fate): The radical acceptance of reality, especially the painful parts. Not passive resignation, but active collaboration with what is.
2. Sympatheia (Interconnectedness): Viewing the organization as a single living organism, where a problem in shipping is as vital as a decision in the boardroom.
3. Memento Mori (Remember You Must Die): Using the awareness of mortality to sharpen focus on what truly matters.

These pillars create a leader who is grounded, systemic, and ruthlessly focussed, a human antifragility engine. The parallel is the servant leadership model: "But whoever would be great among you must be your servant" (Matthew 20:26). The reverse leader serves the truth, even when it hurts.

Case Study 1: The LEGO Turnaround (2004–2015) – Amor Fati in Action
When Jørgen Vig Knudstorp took over LEGO in 2004, the company was weeks from bankruptcy. The previous leadership had refused to acknowledge the digital revolution, clinging to the "purity" of the physical brick. Their failure was a failure of *Amor Fati*, they hated the fate of a changing world.

Knudstorp's first act was a stunning display of Stoic love of fate. He stood before employees and shareholders and stated: "We are going to die. This is a fact. Now, let's love this reality. Let's use this death to ask: what should LEGO become?" This wasn't pessimism; it was liberation. By fully accepting the worst-case scenario, he removed its emotional power. The energy previously spent on denial was redirected into the creative chaos of the 4D process. He loved the fact of their near-death enough to let the old LEGO die, making space for the new one to be born. The result was a 1,100% stock surge and a cultural rebirth.

Case Study 2: Samsung's Burning Galaxy Note 7 (2016) – Sympatheia as Strategy
In 2016, Samsung's flagship Galaxy Note 7 smartphones began spontaneously combusting. The traditional playbook – isolate the problem, blame a supplier, issue a quiet recall, would have been a disaster. Instead, CEO Koh Dong-jin demonstrated *Sympatheia*.

He didn't see the crisis as a "product flaw" isolated to the engineering department. He saw it as a cancer in the entire organism of Samsung. He mandated that every employee, from marketers to accountants, spend a day in a customer service centre, listening to the fear and anger of customers. "The battery is not the problem," he declared. "The problem is the disconnect between our labs and our customers' hands. We are one body. When the hand burns, the whole body feels the pain."

This perspectival shift across the entire company led to the most aggressive recall in tech history and a complete overhaul of their quality control, involving every department. They treated the burn as a nervous system signal, not a localized injury. The crisis became the catalyst for a deeper integration that ultimately strengthened Samsung against future shocks.

Case Study 3: Tata Group's Response to the Mumbai Attacks (2008) – Memento Mori as Moral Compass

When terrorists attacked the Taj Mahal Palace Hotel in Mumbai in 2008, the standard corporate response would have been crisis management: protect the brand, manage the media. But Ratan Tata, chairman of the Tata Group that owned the hotel, embodied *Memento Mori*.

He was photographed not in a boardroom, but in the ashes of the hotel, comforting the family of a slain employee. His first directive was not about rebuilding, but about remembrance: "We will not calculate the cost. We will pay for the education of every child who lost a parent, whether they were an employee or a guest. We will rebuild, but we will first remember why we exist."

This awareness of mortality, of the hotel's, of his employees', sharpened his focus on the company's deepest purpose: service. The decision was economically "irrational," but it forged an unbreakable bond of loyalty with employees and the Indian public. The rebuilt Taj became more than a hotel; it became a symbol of resilience rooted in duty. The value is clear: "Greater love has no one than this, that someone lay down his life for his friends" (John 15:13). Tata was willing to let the profit motive die to save the soul of the company.

The Daily Practices of a Stoic Reverse Leader

Leadership is not a position; it is a daily practice. These are not abstract concepts but concrete exercises:

1. **The Premeditatio Malorum (Premeditation of Evils):** Each morning, spend 5 min vividly imagining everything that could go wrong that day. Visualize your project failing, your key employee quitting, your product being mocked. This is not negative thinking; it is emotional inoculation. By accepting these possibilities before they happen, you rob them of their power to shock you into reactive mode.
2. **The View from Above:** Once a week, spend 10 min visualizing your organization from a satellite's perspective. See the buildings, the people, and the flow

of resources. Then zoom out further, see the city, the country, the planet. This practice instills *Sympatheia*, crushing the ego and reminding you of your small but interconnected role in a vast system.

3. **The Evening Audit:** Each night, ask three questions:
    - *Where did I act according to my principles today?*
    - *Where did I let fear override my judgement?*
    - *What obstacle did I encounter, and how can I use it tomorrow?*

The Reverse Leader's Communication Toolkit

How a Stoic reverse leader speaks and listens:
- They Reframe Failure: Instead of "Whose fault is this?" they ask, "What is this failure trying to teach us?"
- They Embrace Silence: They are comfortable with long pauses in conversation, allowing cognitive friction to breathe and develop.
- They Practice Negative Capability: They can hold two contradictory truths without rushing to resolve them. "The data says cut costs, and our values say protect our team. Let's live in that tension until a third path emerges."
- They Speak Last: In meetings, they state the problem and then listen to every perspective before offering their own. This prevents their authority from short-circuiting the collective intelligence.

Overcoming the Leadership Immune System

Every organization has an immune system designed to reject foreign ideas, including reverse thinking. The leader's most difficult task is to overcome their own senior team's resistance. The tactic is not to overpower, but to reframe.

When a veteran executive says, "This is too risky, we've never done it this way," the reverse leader does not argue. They respond with a perspectival shift: "You're right. Our past success is a treasure. Let's honor it by ensuring it doesn't become our tomb. For the next 10 min, let's role-play as a startup that wants to put us out of business. What would they do?"

This acknowledges the executive's wisdom while gently leading them into a cognitive Dojo where it's safe to experiment.

Worksheet: Your Leadership Obstacle Audit
Identify the largest obstacle facing your team or project and use Stoic principles to reframe it.

Step 1: Name the obstacle
Example: "My team is resistant to adopting a new AI tool. They fear it will make their skills obsolete."

Step 2: Apply amor fati (love of fate)
Do not fight the resistance. Accept it as data. What is the underlying truth? "The truth is that the tool will change their jobs. Their fear is valid. I must love this reality instead of dismissing it."

Step 3: Apply sympatheia (interconnectedness)
How does this resistance signal a larger systemic issue? "This isn't just about one tool. It signals a lack of a clear upskilling path company-wide. The team feels like a disposable part, not a valued organ."

Step 4: Apply memento mori (remember death)
If this resistance continues, what will die? If it's overcome, what new life might emerge? "If this continues, our department will become obsolete. If we overcome it, we could become the company's center of AI excellence."

Step 5: Design a reverse intervention
Based on the above, what is one small action?
"Instead of mandating the tool, I will launch a voluntary 'AI Co-Pilot' pilot program where the most skeptical employee gets dedicated training and becomes the team expert."

Case Study 4: Nintendo's Wii Revolution (2006) – Leading from Humility
In the mid-2000s, the video game industry was in a specs arms race between Sony and Microsoft. The logical path for Nintendo was to compete on power and graphics. Instead, then-CEO Satoru Iwata exhibited profound Stoic humility. He admitted that Nintendo could not win that war.

He asked a reverse thinking question: "What if we stop competing with them? What if we become the 'other', the company for people who don't play video games?" This embrace of their "inferior" position (*amor fati*) led to the Wii, a console that focussed on intuitive motion controls and family fun. It was a massive gamble that required ignoring the core "gamer" demographic. By loving their fate as the underdog and seeing the interconnectedness of the entire family unit (*Sympatheia*), they created a blue ocean market and dramatically expanded the industry.

The Shadow Side: When Reverse Leadership Fails

Reverse leadership is not a magic bullet. It fails when:

1. It Becomes Dogma: The leader becomes attached to "being reverse" and creates conflict for its own sake.
2. It Lacks Compassion: Cognitive friction without psychological safety is just cruelty. The leader must hold the tension between truth and love.
3. It Avoids Decision: The DISTILL phase is crucial. A leader who endlessly explores perspectives without finally making a clear decision creates chaos.

The antidote is the daily practice of humility, constantly asking: "Is this for my ego, or for the good of the whole?"

The Foundation of Service

While Stoicism provides the operating system, the deepest motive for the reverse leader is: service. The leader's role is not to be served, but to serve the truth, the customer, the employee, and the community. This is the ultimate *Memento Mori*: remembering that your authority is temporary and given to you for a purpose larger than yourself.

The reverse leader's integrity check is the question Jesus posed: "For what will it profit a man if he gains the whole world and forfeits his soul?" (Matthew 16:26). A decision that maximizes shareholder value but poisons the environment or exploits workers is a failure of leadership, no matter how "rational" the spreadsheets appear.

Building a Reverse Thinking Organization

Your goal is not just to be a reverse leader, but to build an organization of reverse thinkers. This requires:

- Hiring for Cognitive Flexibility: Look for candidates who can eloquently argue against their own convictions
- Rewarding Intelligent Failure: Create awards for the "Best Lesson from a Well-Executed Failure." – practiced by Steve Bartlett and his team, *The Diary of the CEO*.
- Modelling Vulnerability: As a leader, publicly share your own wrong assumptions and what you learned from them.

This creates a culture where the immune system welcomes new ideas instead of attacking them.

Worksheet: Your Stoic Leadership Manifesto

Distill your leadership philosophy into an actionable manifesto.

Step 1: Core principle (amor fati)
How will you practice loving reality, especially the hard parts?
"I will start every team meeting by having someone share one uncomfortable truth about our project."

Step 2: Systemic view (sympatheia)
How will you reinforce interconnectedness?
"I will require every department head to spend one day per quarter working in a completely different department."

Step 3: Purpose focus (memento mori)
What is the legacy you want your leadership to leave?
"I want to be remembered for building a team that was fearless in telling the truth, even to me."

Step 4: Your reverse action
What is one reverse thinking practice you will implement this month. "I will host a monthly 'Funeral for a Failed Idea' where we autopsy a lost project and celebrate the insights it generated."

The Antifragile Leader in Crisis

The ultimate test of a Stoic reverse leader is a true crisis, a supply chain collapse, a public scandal, and a market crash. The reflexive response is command-and-control. The reverse response is to decentralize thinking.

During the 2011 Thai floods that crippled global hard drive production, Western Digital's CEO did not retreat to a war room. He empowered frontline factory managers to become reverse thinkers, giving them authority to implement local solutions and share learnings across the network in real time. This distributed cognitive friction allowed the company to adapt in dozens of ways simultaneously, recovering faster than competitors who waited for central command. The leader's role was not to have the answers, but to design the system for finding them.

Chapter Takeaways

Mitsubishi's CEO could have fought the nuclear scandal. Instead, he bowed to it, using the energy of public outrage to fuel a transformation. LEGO's Knudstorp could have denied the company's mortality. Instead, he loved it enough to let the old company die.

Remember: The Stoic reverse leader is a paradox, a leader who leads by following the truth, a visionary who seeks to have their vision disproven, a powerful figure who finds strength in humility.

Your leadership journey will be measured not by the absence of obstacles, but by your relationship with them. Will you fight them, fear them, or love them as raw material for growth? The Stoic path is clear: embrace the friction, dissolve your ego, and serve the whole. As Marcus Aurelius wrote, "The best revenge is to be unlike him who performed the injury." The best leadership is to be unlike the arrogant models of the past. Lead backwards, by moving forward through the storm.

Further Reading and Sources

Johnson & Johnson. (1983). *Tylenol crisis internal review.*

Mitroff, I. I. (2005). *Why some companies emerge stronger and better from a crisis.* AMACOM.

Siemens, A. G. (2009). *Annual report and compliance restructuring documentation.*

Toyoda, A. (2010). *Testimony before the U.S. Congress.*

Vogus, T. J., & Sutcliffe, K. M. (2007, October). Organizational resilience: Towards a theory and research agenda. In *2007 IEEE international conference on systems, man and cybernetics* (pp. 3418–3422). Ieee. (useful for Stoic practices → organizational level).

Weick, K. E., & Sutcliffe, K. M. (2001). *Managing the unexpected: Assuring high performance in an age of complexity.* (key literature on mindfulness in HROs). High-reliability/"mindfulness" ideas align with Stoic attentional practices.

Chapter 10
Reverse Thinking in Crises

"Crisis does not remove options; it removes illusions." – Reverse thinking proverb.

The control room at Three Mile Island nuclear facility on March 28, 1979, was a theatre of cognitive collapse. Warning lights flashed contradictory signals. Gauges showed impossible readings. The core was overheating, but the pressure indicators suggested otherwise. The highly trained engineers faced a choice: trust their instruments or trust their instincts. They chose the instruments. That decision nearly caused a catastrophic meltdown that would have rendered Pennsylvania uninhabitable. Their failure wasn't technical, it was cognitive. They lacked the framework to think backward from the unthinkable.

Twenty years later, when the Deepwater Horizon oil rig exploded in the Gulf of Mexico, BP's initial response mirrored Three Mile Island's fatal linearity: contain the leak, protect the stock price, control the narrative. But then something remarkable happened. The company's on-scene coordinator, a junior engineer named Maria Hernandez, made a reverse move. Instead of asking "How do we stop the leak?" she asked: "If this spill continues for 100 days, what will destroy us first? The oil? Or the loss of public trust?" This temporal collapse, thinking from the future catastrophe backward, triggered a complete strategy pivot toward radical transparency and community engagement. This is reverse thinking in crisis: when conventional thinking fails, the ability to think backward, upside down, and inside out becomes your only lifeline.

Why Crises Murder Linear Thought

Crises are not complicated problems; they are complex systems in collapse. Complicated problems have known variables and predictable solutions. Complex systems have emergent properties where the solution changes the problem itself. In a crisis, your brain's prediction machinery, optimized for stable environments, becomes your worst enemy. It defaults to what worked before, in a world that no longer exists.

The Three Mile Island engineers followed their training perfectly. But their training was designed for single-failure scenarios, not the cascade of failures they actually faced. Their linear protocols became cognitive prisons. Reverse thinking shatters these prisons by forcing three emergency mental shifts:

1. Temporal Inversion: Start from the worst-case outcome and work backward

© 2026 Walter de Gruyter GmbH, Berlin | https://doi.org/10.1515/9783112217047-011

2. Perspectival Surrender: Abandon your expert identity and adopt alien viewpoints
3. Ethical Prioritization: Let moral imperatives override operational expediency

The Three Crisis Archetypes

Not all crises are created equal. Reverse thinking tailors its approach to the crisis type:
1. The Avalanche (Sudden Impact): A discrete event that changes everything in moments (e.g. 9/11, Fukushima, and the 2008 financial collapse). Response requires temporal collapse and spatial inversion.
2. The Slow Burn (Creeping Crisis): A problem that develops gradually then crosses a threshold (e.g. the opioid epidemic, the 2008 financial crisis buildup, and climate change). Response requires circular resonance and dimensional stacking.
3. The Wolf in Sheep's Clothing (Crisis Disguised as Success): When your greatest strength becomes your fatal weakness (e.g. Nokia's market share preventing smartphone innovation, WeWork's growth hiding fundamental flaws). Response requires emotional polarity and adversarial metamorphosis.

Case Study 1: The Tylenol Murders (1982) – The Textbook That Wasn't
When seven people died from cyanide-laced Tylenol capsules in Chicago, Johnson & Johnson faced an avalanche crisis. The conventional corporate playbook was clear: minimize liability, recall quietly, and avoid admitting fault. Instead, CEO James Burke applied a stunning reverse move. He didn't think from the present forward ("How do we limit damage?"). He thought from the future backward: "In 20 years, what will we wish we had done today to protect our credibility?"

This temporal collapse led to the now-famous decision: an immediate nationwide recall of 31 million bottles at a cost of $100 million, without waiting for evidence of widespread contamination. The move was considered corporate suicide. Instead, it became the gold standard for crisis management. Burke's reverse thinking transformed a product-tampering catastrophe into a demonstration of integrity that actually strengthened the brand. The value? "For what will it profit a man if he gains the whole world and forfeits his soul?" (Matthew 16:26). Burke chose soul over short-term profit.

Case Study 2: Toyota's Acceleration Crisis (2009–2010) – Fighting the Wrong Battle

When reports surfaced of unintended acceleration in Toyota vehicles, the company's initial response was textbook linear thinking: defend the technology, blame driver error, and protect the reputation for quality. They were fighting the last war, the kind of isolated technical problem they had solved before.

The crisis deepened as deaths mounted and recalls expanded. Toyota was applying spatial thinking in the wrong direction, tracing the problem from their factories forward. The reverse move came when Akio Toyoda, grandson of the founder, took the unprecedented step of testifying before Congress. But his real insight came before the testimony, when he forced his engineers to think backward from the grieving families. "Become the driver whose brakes have failed," he commanded. "What would you want from the company that built your car?"

This perspectival shift revealed that the real crisis wasn't technical, it was relational. Toyota had lost connection with its customers' lived experience. The solution wasn't better PR; it was a complete overhaul of their quality control and communication systems, with customer safety as the absolute priority.

Case Study 3: Siemens' Corruption Scandal (2006–2008) – Embracing the Poison

When Siemens was revealed to have operated a massive, systematic bribery scheme across multiple countries, the company faced institutional death. The standard response, fire a few executives, pay a fine, move on, would have been inadequate. New CEO Peter Löscher made a radical reverse decision: he turned the investigation inward with unprecedented ferocity.

Instead of containing the damage, he amplified it. He hired 500 external lawyers and forensic accountants to investigate every division. He encouraged whistleblowing. He publicly disclosed findings that damaged the company's reputation in the short term. This anticlockwise move, embracing the poison rather than fighting it, was based on a spatial inversion: "The corruption isn't at the edges of our system; it is the system. To heal the body, we must first acknowledge the cancer has metastasized."

The result was a complete cultural transformation that made Siemens a leader in corporate compliance. The crisis became the catalyst for a stronger, more ethical organization.

The Crisis Friction Storm: A Framework for Chaos

When crisis hits, you don't have time for a full 4D Process. You need a rapid-deployment version, the Crisis Friction Storm. This 30-min protocol forces the essential reverse thinking moves under extreme time pressure.

The Four-Question Crisis Framework:
1. Temporal: "What's the worst plausible outcome in 72 h? What would have to be true for that to happen?"
2. Spatial: "If we're the customer/regulator/victim, what are we seeing that we're not telling them?"
3. Emotional: "What does the data say we should do? What does our gut say we must do?"
4. Ethical: "If this decision were on the front page tomorrow, would we be proud or ashamed?"

Case Study 4: The 2010 Chilean Mining Disaster – Temporal Collapse as Salvation

When the San José mine collapsed, trapping 33 miners half a mile underground, the Chilean government faced an impossible situation. Initial assessments indicated rescue would take 4 months, long past the point of survival. The linear approach was to begin drilling and hope.

Then Mining Minister Laurence Golborne made a reverse move. He forced the rescue team to work backward from a successful outcome: "Assume we get them out alive in 60 days. What must be true today to make that possible?"

This temporal collapse revealed that the critical path wasn't the drilling technology, it was maintaining the miners' hope and health during the wait. This insight triggered a massive logistical operation to establish communication, send down supplies, and provide psychological support months before the actual rescue. The result was a miracle that captivated the world, not because of luck, but because of reverse-engineered hope.

The Stoic Crisis Mindset: Amor Fati in the Inferno

Crisis management begins with self-management. The Stoic practices from Chapter 9 become life-or-death disciplines in a crisis:
- **Premeditatio Malorum:** The regular practice of imagining worst-case scenarios inoculates you against panic when they actually happen.
- **The View from Above:** In the midst of chaos, mentally zooming out to see the crisis as one small part of a larger picture prevents catastrophic thinking.
- **Negative Visualization:** Imagining the loss of what you're trying to protect (reputation and market share) can clarify what truly matters.

The parallel is the practice of *kenosis,* self-emptying. In crisis, you must empty yourself of ego, certainty, and the need to be right to be filled with the clarity the situation demands.

Case Study 5: Merck's Vioxx Withdrawal (2004) – When Data Lies
When evidence emerged that Merck's blockbuster painkiller Vioxx increased heart attack risk, the company faced a catastrophic choice: recall a $2.5 billion drug affecting 2 million patients, or wait for more data. The rational, data-driven approach suggested caution: the evidence was statistical, not conclusive.

CEO Raymond Gilmartin made the reverse choice. He applied emotional polarity, forcing the cold data to wrestle with a human perspective: "If one of those statistical percentages was my mother, what would I do?" The answer was immediate and unequivocal. Merck voluntarily withdrew Vioxx in what became the largest drug recall in history. The decision cost billions but preserved the company's integrity, and likely saved thousands of lives. The Stoic virtue? Justice over profit.

Worksheet: Crisis Simulation – The 30-min Drill
Use this worksheet to prepare your team for crises before they happen.

Step 1: Select a crisis scenario
Choose a plausible worst-case scenario for your organization.
Example: "A key manufacturing plant has a fatal accident and environmental spill."

Step 2: Rapid reverse assessment (20 min)

Dimension	Crisis question	Your team's answer
Temporal	*What's the worst outcome in 48 h?*	National media coverage, regulatory shutdown, and employee panic.
Spatial	*What does the victim's family see that we don't?*	They see us as a faceless corporation prioritizing production over safety.
Emotional	*Data says: ____. Gut says: ____.*	Data says secure the site. Gut says go to the hospital immediately.
Ethical	*What would the most ethical version of our company do?*	Shut down all similar operations until safety is verified, regardless of cost.

Step 3: Distill the reverse action (10 min)
Based on the above, what is the one non-obvious action we would take? "Instead of waiting for the investigation, immediately send the CEO to the hospital and announce a voluntary shutdown of all similar operations nationwide."

The Leader's Crisis Transformation

A crisis doesn't just test your thinking, it transforms your leadership. The reverse thinking leader undergoes three metamorphoses during prolonged crisis:

1. From Controller to Context-Setter: They stop trying to control the uncontrollable and instead create the cognitive context for others to solve problems.
2. From Expert to Questioner: They abandon the pretense of having answers and instead ask the revolutionary questions.
3. From Director to Meaning-Maker: They help the organization find purpose in the pain, transforming trauma into growth.

This is the ultimate application of Stoic *amor fati*, not just accepting the crisis, but loving what it can make of you and your organization.

Case Study 6: NASA After Columbia – Dancing with Failure

After the Space Shuttle Columbia disintegrated during re-entry in 2003, NASA faced an existential crisis of confidence. The initial investigation followed the standard linear pattern: find the technical cause (foam striking the wing) and fix it.

But then NASA Administrator Sean O'Keefe made a reverse move. He recognized that the technical failure was a symptom of a cultural disease: the normalization of deviance. He forced the entire organization to apply perspectival shift: "Become the foam. You are a piece of insulation trying to warn the engineers about a fatal flaw they've learned to ignore. What would you say?"

This surreal exercise revealed deeper truths about communication breakdowns and complacency. The crisis became an opportunity for cultural rebirth, making NASA more resilient, transparent, and collaborative. They didn't just fix a technical problem; they transformed their relationship with failure.

When Reverse Thinking Fails in Crisis

Reverse thinking is not a magic bullet. It fails when:

1. It's Applied Too Late: If the organization is already in full panic mode, cognitive overload becomes destructive.

2. It Lacks Authority: Junior employees may see the reverse insight, but without leadership buy-in, it dies.
3. It Becomes Intellectual: In a true emergency, analysis paralysis can be fatal. DISTILL must happen quickly.

The antidote is pre-crisis preparation, making reverse thinking a muscle memory through regular simulation.

The Theology of Crisis

At its deepest level, reverse thinking in crisis touches on theological themes. The crisis becomes a modern-day *via negativam*, the way of negation where truth is found by understanding what something is not. The failure of all conventional solutions creates the emptiness where genuine innovation can emerge.

The narrative of death and resurrection finds its corporate analogue here. The organization must be willing to let its old identity die, its reputation, its business model, its certainty, to be reborn into something more resilient. This is not just strategy; it's corporate kenosis, the self-emptying that makes room for grace.

Building Antifragile Crisis Capacity

Your goal is not just to survive crises, but to build an organization that grows stronger from them. This requires:
- Monthly Reverse Drills: Regular simulations using the Crisis Friction Storm framework.
- Pre-mortems for Major Projects: Before launching, imagine the project has failed spectacularly and work backward to identify vulnerabilities.
- Psychological Safety: Creating an environment where employees can voice uncomfortable truths without fear.

The ultimate test of your reverse thinking capacity is not how you perform in calm waters, but how you dance in the hurricane.

Chapter Takeaways

Three Mile Island's engineers followed their training into disaster. BP's junior engineer asked a backward question that saved the company. Johnson & Johnson's recall seemed like suicide but became legendary. Remember: Crisis murders linear thought. Your standard operating procedures become your death sentence when the world unravels. Reverse thinking in crisis is not a luxury, it's a survival skill. When the next crisis hits, and it will, your first question must be the reverse question: not "How do we fix this?" but "What is this crisis here to teach us?" The obstacle is not just the path; in crisis, the obstacle becomes the teacher. The Stoic insight is profound: the crisis itself is the curriculum. Your job is to be the student humble enough to learn its brutal lessons. As the ancient proverb whispers: "Smooth seas do not make skillful sailors." Your organization's greatest growth awaits not in the calm, but in the storm. Have the courage to think backward when everyone else is charging forward. Your survival depends on it.

Further Reading and Sources

Comfort, L. K. (2007). *Crisis management in hindsight: Cognition, communication, coordination, and control*. Public Administration Review. (Links cognition & coordination in large-scale crise).
Weick, K. E. (1993). *The collapse of sensemaking in organizations: The Mann Gulch disaster*. Administrative Science Quarterly. (Case study on how sensemaking fails in crisis).

Chapter 11
The Reverse Thinker's Field Manual

"In the field, elegance is a liability. Clarity saves lives." – Reverse thinking proverb

Why This Chapter Exists: How to Deploy the Framework When Reality Will Not Wait

Up to this point, this book has deliberately resisted simplification. You have been asked to tolerate ambiguity, friction, and multidimensional tension because real systems demand it. However, leaders do not fail because they lack insight. They fail because they misapply insight under pressure.

This chapter exists for moments when:
- Time is compressed
- Authority is contested
- Stakes are asymmetrical
- And overthinking becomes as dangerous as underthinking

The field manual is not a summary of the book. It is a deployment guide, designed for use *inside* meetings, crises, and irreversible decisions.

If the rest of this book trains perception, this chapter trains judgement.

Section I: When to Apply Which Dimension

Reverse thinking fails when all dimensions are applied indiscriminately. Mastery lies in knowing which lens unlocks movement in a given context.

Below is a situational deployment map.

1 Use Temporal Flow When the Organization Is Calm but Wrong

Signal
- Metrics look stable
- Leadership expresses confidence
- Frontline discomfort is dismissed as noise

© 2026 Walter de Gruyter GmbH, Berlin | https://doi.org/10.1515/9783112217047-012

Risk
–   Linear extrapolation masquerading as strategy

Deploy Temporal Flow When
–   Past success is used as evidence of future safety
–   Strategy is justified primarily through trend continuation

Field Question
"If this decision leads to failure three years from now, what will future leaders say was obvious today?"

Do Not Use When
–   The system is already in acute crisis
–   Immediate containment is required

Temporal flow destabilizes comfort; it should not destabilize emergency response.

2 Use Spatial Axis When Execution Is "Correct" but Outcomes Are Wrong

Signal
–   Every function is performing its role
–   KPIs are being met locally
–   System-level results are deteriorating

Risk
–   Fragmented optimization hiding systemic failure

Deploy Spatial Axis When
–   Accountability conversations go in circles
–   No single team "owns" the problem

Field Question
"Where does the pain actually land, and what does it trace back to?"

Do Not Use When
–   The problem is clearly isolated and technical
–   The root cause is already verified

Spatial inversion is diagnostic, not decorative.

3 Use Emotional Polarity When Data Is Abundant but Conviction Is Absent

Signal
- Analysis paralysis
- Excessive modelling with no decision
- Low-energy agreement

Risk
- Emotional avoidance disguised as rationality

Deploy Emotional Polarity When
- Teams converge too quickly
- "Reasonable" options all feel hollow

Field Question
"What option feels irrational but morally or intuitively necessary?"

Do Not Use When
- The system is already emotionally inflamed
- Ego or identity threat is driving conflict

Emotional polarity is a controlled collision, not an emotional release.

4 Use Dynamism When the System Is Frozen by Risk Management

Signal
- Heavy reliance on governance
- Fear of precedent
- Innovation framed as threat

Risk
- Stability becoming decay

Deploy Dynamism When
- Protecting the system matters more than improving it
- "Best practice" is used as a shield

Field Question

"If this system had to survive radical disruption tomorrow, what would it abandon today?"

Do Not Use When
- Trust is low
- Psychological safety has not been established

Chaos without trust produces fear, not insight.

5 Use Circular Resonance When Small Issues Keep Reappearing

Signal
- Recurring "minor" complaints
- Local fixes that never stick

Risk
- Underestimating micro-level erosion

Deploy Circular Resonance When
- Culture problems are labelled as "soft"
- Leadership dismisses operational irritants

Field Question

"If this small issue scaled across the system, what would it destroy?"

Do Not Use When
- The issue is genuinely isolated and non-repeating

Circular analysis is about patterns, not anecdotes.

6 Use Perspectival Shift When Stakeholders Talk Past One Another

Signal
- Moral stalemates
- Competing narratives
- Identity-based resistance

Risk
- Each side optimizing its own logic

Deploy Perspectival Shift When
- No amount of explanation changes minds
- Incentives alone fail

Field Question
"If I were the 'other' in this system, what would feel invisible, threatened, or non-negotiable?"

Do Not Use When
- The goal is speed, not understanding
- Authority must be exercised immediately

Perspective is powerful, but slow.

7 Use Dimensional Stacking Only When the Problem Is Truly Existential

Signal
- Trade-offs feel morally unacceptable
- Any single solution creates secondary collapse

Risk
- False binaries
- Strategic despair

Deploy Dimensional Stacking When
- The problem spans time, ethics, systems, and identity
- Incrementalism is insufficient

Field Question
"What hybrid solution only becomes visible when multiple dimensions are held simultaneously?"

Do Not Use When
- The decision is routine
- Overengineering would create delay

Stacking is rare. That is why it works.

Section II: What Not to Do (Misuse Patterns)

Most failures of reverse thinking are not conceptual, they are behavioural.

Misuse 1: Dimensional Maximalism

Applying all dimensions at once to simple problems.

Symptom
- Endless workshops
- No action

Correction
- Match dimensional complexity to problem complexity.

Misuse 2: Intellectual Theatre

Using the language of reverse thinking to signal sophistication.

Symptom
- Elegant framing with no intervention
- Insight without consequence

Correction
- Every insight must change a behaviour, process, or decision.

Misuse 3: Ethical Exceptionalism

Justifying harm through "higher-order thinking."

Symptom
- "The system requires this"
- Responsibility diffusion

Correction
- If a decision cannot be defended to the most affected party, it is incomplete.

Misuse 4: Premature Stacking

Attempting synthesis before tension has done its work.

Symptom
- Forced compromises
- Conceptual vagueness

Correction
- Let collisions mature before resolution.

Section III: Warning Signs You Are Misapplying the Framework

Stop and recalibrate if you notice:
- Reverse thinking being used to avoid decisions
- Senior leaders monopolizing dimensional language
- Junior voices disappearing rather than emerging
- Ethics framed as "constraints" rather than signals
- Insight increasing while responsibility decreases

These are not execution problems. They are integrity failures.

Section IV: A 15-Min Field Deployment Protocol

When time is scarce, use this sequence:
1. **Name the failure mode** (not the solution)
2. **Select one dominant dimension** only
3. **Ask one destabilizing question**
4. **Identify the smallest irreversible action**
5. **Assign ownership before consensus**

If no action emerges, stop. Insight without movement is indulgence.

Closing: The Discipline of Restraint

Reverse thinking is not about thinking more. It is about thinking only what matters, at the moment it matters, with the humility to stop when clarity arrives.

Frameworks do not save systems.

Judgement does.

This field manual is not a guarantee of correctness. It is a defence against blindness.

Use it sparingly.

Use it honestly.

And remember: the most dangerous misuse of any framework is using it to avoid moral responsibility.

Conclusion: The Unfinished Mind

"The moment thinking feels complete is the moment it stops protecting you." – Reverse thinking proverb.

They told you the story of Nokia as a cautionary tale. They were wrong. Nokia was not a failure; it was a sacrifice, a burnt offering on the altar of a dying era. Its corpse became the fertile soil from which a new way of thinking now grows. You have journeyed through the wreckage of linear thought, witnessed the resurrection of Lego, danced in the friction storms of Airbnb, and learned to think like a glacier with Patagonia. But this book was never about them. It is about the unfinished mind waiting to be born in you.

The cognitive revolution does not begin in boardrooms or innovation labs. It begins in the silent space between your thoughts, the moment you choose discomfort over delusion, curiosity over certainty, service over security. You stand at the precipice of a world where AI rewrites reality faster than regulators can type, where loyalty is an algorithm away from evaporation, where the only sustainable advantage is the ability to think in directions that don't yet have names. This is not a threat. This is your invitation to become more human than you were programmed to be.

The Antifragile Awakening

Reverse thinking is not a methodology. It is metabolic. It changes how you process reality itself. Like the immune system that grows stronger after exposure to pathogens, the reverse thinker thrives on volatility. Remember Pfizer's vaccine team, turning −70 °C logistics from crisis into advantage? That same antifragility now lives in you, the ability to convert obstacles into fuel.

Your generational advantage is profound: you have never known stability. You are native to disruption. The pandemic, the digital transformation, the gig economy, these were not interruptions to your development. They were your training ground. While corporate veterans cling to best practices like life racks in a hurricane, you have been learning to swim in the storm. Reverse thinking simply gives language to what you already know in your bones: that certainty is the enemy of evolution.

© 2026 Walter de Gruyter GmbH, Berlin | https://doi.org/10.1515/9783112217047-013

The Seven Silent Revolutions

As you leave these pages, seven quiet revolutions are already unfolding within you:
1. Temporal Liberation: You no longer see time as a straight line but as a fluid dimension to be collapsed and expanded.
2. Spatial Fluidity: You trace problems backward from their point of impact, finding truth in the upstream journey.
3. Emotional Alchemy: You welcome the duel between data and intuition, knowing synthesis births wisdom.
4. Chaos Collaboration: You dance with disruption as a partner, not an enemy.
5. Microscopic Vision: You see the universe in a grain of sand, the tiny flaw that reveals the systemic crack.
6. Perspectival Shapeshifting: You wear alien eyes as naturally as your own.
7. Cognitive Fusion: You stack dimensions until new realities emerge from the friction.

These are not skills to be mastered. They are muscles to be exercised, and they atrophy faster than you think.

The Unfinished Manifesto

This book ends where your true work begins. Carry these truths as your compass:
1. Your Title is a Tombstone: The moment you identify as "expert," "manager," or "specialist," you join Nokia in the graveyard. Stay fluid. You are a verb, not a noun.
2. Discomfort is Your North Star: If your strategy doesn't terrify you, it's obsolete. Seek the friction where opposites spark fire.
3. Serve or Perish: Your legacy will not be measured in profit but in uplift. Always ask: "Who does this truly serve?"

The most dangerous thought you can have is "I understand." The moment you believe you've grasped reverse thinking; you have lost it. The unfinished mind is perpetually curious, relentlessly adaptable, and humble enough to know that every solution is temporary.

Your Battle Plan for the Cognitive Revolution

This is not self-help. This is a declaration of war against the finished minds ruling our crumbling institutions. Your mission begins now:

- At Dawn: Run the perspective ladder. Become your future corpse → your fiercest critic → a silent stakeholder (a river, an algorithm).
- In Meetings: Ignite miniature friction storms. "For the next four minutes, everyone argue against your deepest conviction."
- At Midnight: Ask Bourla's distill question: "What one action honours 80% of the truths we've uncovered?"

The revolution will not be televised. It will happen in the quiet moments: when a CEO becomes a janitor for a day, when an intern role-plays as the AI that might replace her, when you choose the uncomfortable truth over the convenient lie.

The Ghosts of Future Past

Look ahead 5 years. Two versions of you exist in parallel futures.

In one, you followed the straight lines. You optimized, streamlined, and coloured inside the borders. You became very good at playing a game that no longer exists. The world became stranger and more fractured around you, until one day you realized you were speaking a language nobody understood anymore.

In the other future, you became a cognitive contortionist. You burned the box and danced in the ashes. You failed spectacularly and learned voraciously. You led not with answers but with revolutionary questions. When the next crisis hit, the one nobody saw coming, you were the calm in the storm because you had learned to think like the storm itself.

Which ghost will visit your present self? The choice is made not in one grand gesture, but in the small, daily acts of cognitive courage.

The Covert Covenant

Woven through these pages is a thread older than Stoicism, more revolutionary than any business strategy. It is the ancient idea that true power lies in service, that the last shall be first, that the meek shall inherit the earth. Reverse thinking is ultimately a spiritual practice disguised as a cognitive tool. It is the daily discipline of ego death in service of a truth larger than yourself.

When you choose the irrational path that serves the customer, when you embrace the perspective of the marginalized, when you prioritize purpose over profit, you are participating in a covert covenant. You are building the kind of world that might one day be worthy of your children. This is not business. This is soulcraft.

The Unfinished Symphony

The reverse thinking framework is complete, but your journey is not. What comes next?
- The Reverse Thinking Dojo: An online community where practitioners host live Friction Storms and Rolling Role-Plays on real-world challenges.
- The Antifragile Leadership Intensive: A 90-day programme for transforming entire teams into Reverse Thinking organisms.
- The Unfinished Mind Newsletter: Injections of cognitive adrenaline, case studies, worksheets, and provocations.

But these are just scaffolds. The real work happens in the space between your thoughts, the moment before you default to the known, when you choose the uncharted path instead.

Your First Reverse Action

The straight lines are gone. The revolution begins now. Your first mission:
1. Tear out the final worksheet (or screenshot it).
2. Break One Linear Rule Today: Send the email that terrifies you. Map your career backward from your deathbed. Become your office plant and observe what you see.
3. Join the Unfinished: Share your breakthrough at #ReverseThinkingRevolution.

This is not the end. This is your activation.

> "They told you to think outside the box. This was a lie. Burn the box. Dance in the ashes. Forge new worlds from the fire."

The unfinished mind is your birthright. Stay hungry. Stay fluid. Stay antifragile.

The revolution continues at #ReverseThinkingRevolution

Worksheet: The Revolution Starter Kit

Step 1: Your linear funeral
What "straight line" thinking are you ready to bury today?
    Example: "My belief that a 5-year plan will protect me."

Step 2: Your first reverse intervention
What one reverse thinking dimension will you weaponize this week?
    "I will practice Temporal Collapse: writing my project's failure headline from 2028."

Step 3: Your covert covenant
Who will your thinking serve beyond yourself?
    "My team's morale, our customers' dignity, the environment my children will inherit."

Step 4: Your unfinished promise
Complete this sentence: "I will stay unfinished by . . ."
    ". . . asking one stupid question every day and embracing the silence that follows."

Share your completed worksheet with #ReverseThinkingRevolution. The most provocative entries will be featured in the next evolution.

Further Reading and Sources

Taleb, N. N. (2018). *Skin in the game*. Random House.
Popper, K. R. (1963). *Conjectures and refutations*. Routledge.
Berlin, I. (1993). *The hedgehog and the fox*. Ivan R. Dee.

Index

© 2026 Walter de Gruyter GmbH, Berlin | https://doi.org/10.1515/9783112217047-014